Links of Light: The Golden Chain

A child's version of The Naqshbandi Sufi Way

By
Shaykh Muhammad Hisham Kabbani

Adapted By
Karima Sperling

Illustrated By
Alia Sperling Nazeer

Naqshbandi-Haqqani Sufi Order of America

© 2009 Naqshbandi-Haqqani Sufi Order of America

All rights reserved. No part of this book may be reproduced, stored in a retrieval system, or transmitted in any form, or by any means, electronic, mechanical, photocopying, or otherwise, without the written permission of the Naqshbandi-Haqqani Sufi Order.

Published and Distributed by:
Naqshbandi-Haqqani Sufi Order of America
17195 Silver Parkway, #201
Fenton, MI 48430 USA
Tel: (888) 278-6624
Fax: (810) 815-0518
Email: staff@naqshbandi.org

Library of Congress Control Number: To be assigned
ISBN: 978-1-930409-68-2

On the Internet, please visit:
www.naqshbandi.org
and
www.isn1.net
for more titles in Islamic spirituality and traditional scholarship.

Dedication

We begin as all things began and continue to be,

In The Name Of Allah, The Most Merciful, The Most Compassionate.

We ask Allah to enoble our humble efforts with His grace and bless them with usefulness in this world. May some of the light carried by His saintly servants be reflected in the following pages.

This book is dedicated to Mawlana Shaykh Nazim al-Haqqani, who for the last 35 years has been the possessor of the light and the supreme master of our time. In all these years he has never tired of reaching out to all the people of the world with love and concern, inviting them to come and take his hand and to follow him to safety and happiness. May Allah shower him with spiritual gifts from His heavenly treasures and give him health and ease in this world. We pray that Allah continue to grant him long life and that we may live in the light of his love for a very, very long time.

This book is also dedicated to Shaykh Muhammad Hisham Kabbani, Shaykh Nazim's deputy in America, who authored the amazing volume from which this small children's version was derived. He was the first to put into English a collection of some of the wisdom of the classic saints of Islam. By his constant and complete dedication to his Shaykh and his Lord, he sets before us a shining example of what it means to follow their Way. We thank him for his example, his light, and his untiring efforts to teach us.

Thanks

To Allah Almighty Who gave us ears to hear with, eyes to see with, and hands to do with, thank You! Thank You for lighting our way with the Shaykhs and the Saints. All light is from You and to You is our journey.

Thank you to Shaykh Nazim and all his family for their help and inspiration. May Allah bless all of them in this life and the next.

Thank you to all my family for their patience and support; to Munir for his advice on all levels; to Alia for her wonderful drawings and continual feedback; to Aminah for her computer skills, proofreading and formatting.

Thank you to Taher Siddiqui for getting the book ready for publishing.

Thank you to the Mahmoud Shelton Family for their support, encouragement and advice.

Thank you to Karima and Bahauddin Kylberg for their proofreading and support.

How To Use This Book

The purpose of this book is to introduce children to the Shaykhs of the Golden Chain. It is meant to follow two previous books, <u>My Little Lore of Light</u> (stories of the Prophets), and <u>The Light of Muhammad (sas)</u>, (a biography). As such, it is a continuation of the story of the Light from the time of the Prophet (sas) until the present day.

The Prophet (sas) said, as recorded in Hadith, "To remember righteous men brings mercy to the believers." Remembering saintly people, even if only by mentioning their names, brings great blessings. To recall them is like calling to them and we are assured that they will answer us.

The aim of each chapter is to provide the reader with a story or saying that will make each Shaykh memorable. This was not always an easy task since it was of necessity dependant upon the material available. Sometimes this material was inappropriate because of its complexity and sometimes there was just very little to choose from.

At the end of each chapter blessings are asked for all of the Shaykhs up until that point. This, I hope, will aid the reader in memorizing the list, one Shaykh at a time. It could be used as a sort of memory game. The form of this list is the one passed down to us from our Grandshaykh, Abdullah ad-Daghestani (q).

Hidden Treasure In The Pictures

The purpose of each picture is to aid the reader in remembering. In addition, within each picture is a game. Hidden within the lines of the picture is the name of the Prophet Muhammad (sas) written in Arabic, in several different calligraphic styles, such as: محمد or محمد . Each picture has a number beside the name of the shaykh indicating how many times the name of the Prophet (sas) is hidden inside that drawing. On the cover picture you will see the names high-lighted in order to serve as an example.

Salutations

Following the name of a prophet or saint is an abbreviation that represents a blessing in Arabic. It becomes cumbersome to read it out loud and is usually not said when reciting the list of the Shaykhs of the Golden Chain. It is written, however, in order to be consistent and respectful. It can be left out when reading out loud, or better yet, said quietly on the heart. It is a good thing to teach children these phrases of respect.

(sas) –sallallahu alayhi was-salim. May Allah give him peace and blessings. This phrase is used for the Prophet Muhammad (sas) as ordered in the Quran.

(as) – alayhi salam. Peace be upon him. This is used for all other prophets.

(ahs) – alayha salam. Peace be upon her. This is used for female members of the Prophet's (sas) family and those women like Maryam (ahs), the mother of Isa (as).

(ahums) –alayhum salam. Peace be upon them.

(ra) – radhi Allahu 'anhu. May Allah be pleased with him. This is used for the companions of the prophets.

(rah) – radhi Allahu 'anha. May Allah be pleased with her. This is used for the female companions of the prophets.

(rahum) – radhi Allahu 'anhum. May Allah be pleased with them.

(q) – qadas Allahu sirrahu. May Allah sanctify his secret. This is used for saints and shaykhs.

(qha) – qadas Allahu sirraha. May Allah sanctify her secret. This is used for female saints and Shaykhas.

    (qhum) – qadas Allahu sirrahum. May Allah sanctify their secret.

Table of Contents

Dedication..iii
Thanks..iv
How To Use This Book..v
0 The Light and the Secret...2
1 An-Nabi Muhammad (sas)..10
2 Abu Bakr as-Siddiq (ra)...18
3 Salman al-Farsi (ra)...24
4 Qasim ibn Muhammad ibn Abu Bakr (ra)...30
5 Jafar as-Sadiq (ra)...34
6 Tayfur Abu Yazid al-Bistami (q)...38
7 Abul Hasan al-Kharqani (q)..44
8 Abu Ali al-Farmadi (q)..48
9 Abu Ya'qub Yusuf al-Hamadani (q)..52
10 Abul Abbas al-Khidr (as)..58
11 Abdul Khaliq al-Ghujdawani (q)...64
12 Arif ar-Rivgari (q)...70
13 Mahmoud al-Injir al-Faghnawi (q)..74
14 Ali ar-Ramitani, Azizan (q)...78
15 Muhammad Baba as-Samasi (q)...82
16 Sayyid Amir Kulal (q)...86
17 Muhammad Bahauddin Shah Naqshband (q).....................................90
18 Alauddin al-Attar (q)...96
19 Ya'qub al-Charkhi (q)..100
20 Ubaydallah al-Ahrar (q)..106
21 Muhammad az-Zahid (q)..112
22 Darwish Muhammad (q)...116
23 Muhammad al-Amkanaki (q)..120

24 Muhammad al-Baqi Billah (q)..124

25 Ahmad al-Faruqi as-Sirhindi (q)..128

26 Muhammad Ma'sum (q)...134

27 Muhammad Sayfuddin (q)..138

28 Nur Muhammad al-Badawani (q)...142

29 Shamsuddin Habib Allah (q)..146

30 AbdAllah Ad-Dahlawi, Shah Ghulam Ali (q)..152

31 Khalid Al-Baghdadi (q)..158

32 Ismail ash-Shirwani (q)..164

33 Khas Muhammad ash-Shirwani (q)..170

34 Muhammad Effendi al-Yaraghi (q)..174

35 Jamaluddin al-Ghumuqi al-Husayni (q)...180

36 Abu Ahmad as-Sughuri (q)..186

37 Abu Muhammad al-Madani (q)..192

38 Shaykh Sharafuddin ad-Daghestani (q)..198

39 Abdallah al-Faiz ad-Daghestani (q)...204

40 Shaykh Nazim Adil al-Haqqani (q)..210

2 Links of Light: The Golden Chain

The Light and The Secret

In the beginning, before there was time and space, before there was even light and darkness, there was Allah and only Allah.

Then Allah decided to create the worlds and everything in them. This creation would act as a mirror to reflect some of the indescribably beautiful and majestic qualities of its Creator. This act of reflection is what we mean when we talk about worshiping God or serving Him. It is our purpose in life and the reason for our creation. We must try to reflect, as best we can, our individual portion of the light, given to us by the One from Whose light we were made. Allah is the light. We are the reflections. Allah is the Master. We are His servants.

One of the first beings Allah Almighty created was the Pen (as) and He ordered it to write the will of its Lord across the emptiness. The first thing Allah ordered the Pen (as) to write was: *La ilaha illa Allah, Muhammad Rasulullah.* There is no god but the One God and Muhammad (sas) is His Messenger.

The Pen (as), because it is a kind of angel, could speak and it asked its Lord, "Who is this Muhammad (sas) whose name I have written beside Your Holy Name?" Allah answered the Pen (as) that Muhammad (sas) was to be the created being in whom the meaning of the phrase, *La ilaha illa Allah*, would be most perfectly reflected. He would be created to be the perfect worshipper, the perfect servant. He was to be Allah's beloved and for his sake Allah would create all the rest of the worlds in their extraordinary beauty and complexity. This was the origin from which everything else was made.

Then Allah Almighty created the light of Muhammad (sas) from His own radiant light. This light of Muhamamd (sas) was hung from the branches of the Tree of Certainty in the highest-most Heaven. There it shone and pulsed with the praises of its Creator for more time than we could ever count. If the light of Allah is like the sun, then Muhammad (sas) is like the moon. The moon softly reflects the light of the sun making it possible for us to gaze on it directly without being blinded.

From this light of Muhammad (sas) Allah then made, first the lights of all the prophets, then the lights of all the saints, then the lights of all believers, and last of all the very dim lights of those who would refuse to believe at all. To our eyes sunlight appears to be clear and white. However, we know that when it passes through a crystal prism it breaks apart and we are able to see that its white light is actually made up of all the colors of the rainbow. In just such a way the light of the Prophet (sas) contains within its clear, white, brightness all of the individual lights of each member of the whole of creation.

Allah then made the soul of Muhammad (sas) and from it He made the souls of the rest of creation. As He said in the Holy Quran, O men, "your creation and your re-creation after death are only as a single soul" (31:28). That single soul is the soul of Muhammad (sas).

Although the Prophet's (sas) light and soul were created first, his body was created much later. He is called the "first" because he was created first. He is called the "last" because he was not born into this world until after all the other prophets had already come and gone.

In 570 CE Allah placed the light and soul of Muhammad (sas) in the body of a beautiful baby, born to a young noblewoman in the desert of Arabia. He nursed, he played, he laughed, as all children do but inside his heart he carried the perfect secret of *La ilaha illa Allah* as no other children do.

At first only the natural creation recognized his secret. The hard ground grew soft under his feet to cushion his steps. The soft sand grew firm to support him. The trees bent and bowed themselves before him and even made way for him to pass. The seemingly lifeless stones spoke to give him greetings. The wild birds and animals approached him shyly and gently just for the chance to feel his touch. Even the clouds followed above him in an effort to serve him by providing shade. It took men a longer time to sense his secret. But little by little they also were drawn to him until he was respected and honored above others in his small city.

The Prophet (sas) lived a normal life among his people. He married. He had four beautiful daughters, and two sons who died as babies. He worked. He ate and hosted guests. He served his community by leading them in making fair decisions and by protecting the weak. He was an honored and respected leader. During all that time his heart remained connected and in close company with his Lord. Never did his daily life distract him from remembering the One Who created the universe and everything in it.

After forty years the Archangel Jibrail (as) was sent to deliver the first verses of the Quran, Allah's book of guidance and inspiration for all of mankind. The Prophet (sas) began to share openly some of the light that overflowed from the great secret securely hidden in his loving heart. More and more people were drawn to this light and gathered around him. Many other people, however, turned away in pride and jealousy and refused to hear or see. He found himself attacked on all sides, even by those who had been close to him. Their anger and jealousy turned violent. Some even wanted to kill him. Allah protected and comforted His beloved with a circle of remarkable men, whom we call his Companions, the foremost among them being Sayyidina Abu Bakr (ra), Sayyidina Ali (ra), Sayyidina Umar (ra) and Sayyidina Uthman (ra).

6 Links of Light: The Golden Chain

As the physical world around him became more dangerous and hostile, the spiritual world burst into bloom. One night as he was resting in the courtyard of an aunt, the Archangel Jibrail (as) was sent by Allah to awaken him. This night was to be the fulfillment of his great destiny. Allah called the Prophet Muhammad (sas) to come to visit Him.

In one night Jibrail (as) accompanied the Prophet (sas) from Mecca to Jerusalem. From there they mounted a jeweled ladder that climbed up into the heavens. The Prophet (sas) traveled through the vast expanses of the heavens and was shown the wondrous creations of his Lord. He saw angels of every size and description praising, praying to, and honoring their Creator. Allah showed him all of the created beings, each one of them dressed with a special and unique quality from its Lord, no two of them the same. The Prophet (sas) was amazed and awestruck. Allah asked him to accept, as a gift, all of this beautiful creation. At the end of time, when everything will return to its Lord, this creation will also need to be returned in the same perfect condition in which it was given. The Prophet (sas) accepted the gift and the heavy responsibility that came with it.

Then Allah showed him the many forms of darkness and misery into which these beautiful creations could fall. Muhammad (sas) remembered his promise to return the gift in the same condition as he had received it. He asked his Lord to give him helpers in this overwhelming task. Allah showed His Prophet (sas) the spirits of the men and women who would be his helpers. At all times there are always seven thousand and seven (7,007) Naqshbandi saints helping to guide and protect the whole of creation. When any one of these saints passes away another takes his place, and we are never, ever, left without their help and guidance.

Then Allah made the spirit of Abu Bakr (ra) appear beside the Prophet (sas). Muhammad (sas) ordered Abu Bakr (ra) to call the souls of each of the 7,007 Naqshbandi saints from every time period and with them all their followers. They came one by one into the Divine Presence to receive from their Lord His gift of light and blessings.

Within two lengths of an archer's bow the Prophet (sas) approached Allah Almighty. No creature has ever been so close before or since. Not even the Archangel Jibrail (as) could accompany the Prophet (sas) to this exalted place. Allah poured into the Prophet's (sas) heart such wondrous secrets and amazing lights that they could not be described in words nor could they even be shared with every one of the Companions. They could only be passed from one heart to another heart that had been carefully prepared to receive such a gift.

10 Links of Light: The Golden Chain

The Night Journey of an-Nabi, Muhammad (sas)

1
An-Nabi Muhammad (sas)

When the Prophet (sas) returned from his journey through the heavens he knew the secrets of creation with more than the eyes of his heart. He knew them with every sense of his body and soul. He had heard and seen, touched and tasted, all of creation, its past and its future. He had been in the presence of Allah Almighty and witnessed His power and His majesty, His glory and His beauty. It was not easy for him to leave the paradise gardens and the glorious presence of Allah in order to return to this difficult and painful world. He returned only out of love for us.

He returned in order to help those of us who are stuck believing that what our eyes see is all there is, that the misery and pain, war and poverty in the world around us are without purpose, justice, meaning, or end. The Prophet (sas) brought with him light to dispel this darkness, love to dispel this despair. He knew how to live life in a healthy way that brings peace to the heart and to the world around. Most importantly, he knew how to gently guide each individual person to the way that would bring him safely home to Allah.

Muhammad (sas) was created by Allah to be an example for us. His every word and every action is a lesson for those who can understand. His companions gathered around him as little children at the feet of their mother. They watched his every move and every step and they tried to be like him. Some people came from far away and only sat with him for a few days or months. Some people spent their whole lives in his company. There were even a remarkable few who, like us, never met him in person at all but who connected with him in a spiritual way.

When the Prophet (sas) was dying he had a very high fever and began to sweat until his robes became soaking wet. He called for Sayyidina Umar (ra) and Sayyidina Ali (ra) to come to him. He told them that after his death they must take his sweat-drenched outer robe and give it to a man whom he called Uways al-Qarni (ra) who lived in the mountains of Yemen herding his sheep. This man was his mother's only child. Because she could not bear to part with her son, he never left her, not even for a short visit to the Prophet (sas) in Medina as he longed to do. But the Prophet (sas) knew Uways (ra) because Allah can bring people's souls and hearts together even when their bodies remain apart.

When the blessed Prophet (sas) died he was buried in the clothes he was wearing except for the outer cloak which Ali (ra) and Umar (ra) took in order to fulfill the Prophet's (sas) order. They went together into the hills asking everyone they met for the whereabouts of Uways al-Qarni (ra). No one had ever heard of a shepherd by that name but they directed the two companions to a shepherd whom they knew as Abdullah. Maybe he would know of the man they were looking for.

They found the man called Abdullah sitting on a hill with his back towards them. As they came near, without looking at them or even turning his head, he said, "Welcome Ali (ra) and welcome Umar (ra). Have you brought what belongs to me?" Immediately the Companions handed him the Prophet's (sas) cloak. He stood up and kissed it and put it around his shoulders while saying, "I accept, I accept, I accept."

Then Uways (ra), for that is who he was, turned to Ali (ra) and Umar (ra) and asked them a question they found very strange. "Did you ever see the Prophet (sas)?" he asked. Both Sayyidina Ali (ra) and Sayyidina Umar (ra) had lived their whole lives in the company of the Prophet (sas). Umar (ra) thought that since Uways (ra) had never met the Prophet (sas) he wanted a physical description and he began to tell him of the Prophet's (sas) handsome appearance and gentle manner.

Uways (ra) shook his head and asked Ali (ra) the same question. "Did you ever see the Prophet of God (sas)?" Ali (ra) knew that Uways (ra) was asking about a different way of seeing. He answered, "Yes, one time I saw the Prophet of God (sas). I saw that from his

feet to his waist he filled all the seven Earths and from his waist to his neck he filled all the seven heavens. I could not see his head because it was too high up, but I knew it reached all the way to the Throne of God and I knew that he was at the heart of the Divine Presence."

"Yes," said Uways (ra), "You truly saw the Prophet of God (sas)." Then Uways (ra) explained to them that as he lay dying the Prophet (sas) was continuously praying to Allah to forgive and to clean every person who ever lived or will live. Each drop of his precious sweat was made for an individual person and it has the power to wash away whatever mistakes or unkind things that person may have done. Uways (ra) was given the responsibility to pass the secret of this cloak and its drops of mercy to the saints whose job it would be to guide and care for each of those individuals. That secret and the ability to wash away mistakes, continues to be passed from teacher to follower down through the ages.

All the Prophet's (sas) Companions, whatever their ability to see, loved their Prophet (sas) with all their heart and soul. They dedicated their lives and their property to his service. They left their homes and families to follow him. They laid down their lives to fight behind him and to protect him.

When the Prophet (sas) washed in preparation for prayer, his Companions caught the water and drank it for its power of healing and blessing. They kissed his hands and his feet when they got the chance. If a hair of his beard or head became loose they collected it and kept it to pass on to their children. Pieces of his clothing and even his old worn-out shoes were treasured above gold and jewels. They asked his advice about all their daily affairs and accepted his judgment when they differed. Every word he spoke, every action he made they watched and remembered, each person according to his ability.

Abu Bakr (ra) recorded all he witnessed in two books, one he handed down to us, one his daughter saw him destroy. Another Companion, Abu Hurayra (ra), said "The Prophet (sas) poured into my heart two kinds of knowledge: one I have shared with people, the other, if I were to share it, would cause some of them to want to cut my throat." One kind of knowledge was written and passed on to everyone. But there is another kind of knowledge, just like there is another kind of seeing, and it can only be passed to those who are able to understand and appreciate it. This kind of knowledge is kept secret or hidden because it can be misunderstood by those who are not ready to receive it. In reality it is hidden only by our own blindness. This knowledge continues to be passed from heart to heart among the saintly followers of the Prophet (sas).

With the support of his Lord, the Prophet (sas) had struggled to deliver Allah's message until all those who had opposed him, freely accepted Allah as their Lord. Those who had been his most bitter enemies now came to him humbly to be forgiven and welcomed into the new community of Islam. After only sixty-three years on this earth Allah took His Prophet (sas) to Him for eternity. The day the Prophet (sas) died was the saddest day on earth since the creation of man.

When the Prophet (sas) left this world, however, he did not disappear. He is still present for those given the eyes and the heart to see. He is alive in his grave. His soul is still praying for us all and watching over us because he has a commitment to His Lord to return our souls shining and sparkling like the day they were created. In addition, by their connection to the Prophet (sas), his helpers, the saints, represent him in this world to guide us and support us. By sitting with them it is as if we are sitting in the company of the beloved Prophet (sas) himself. By following them we are following in his blessed footsteps, and by serving them we may still dedicate our lives to the service of Muhammad *Rasulullah* (sas).

This book contains a few of the stories of forty of the most distinguished saints. Their hearts were able to contain the secret of the Prophet (sas) and pass it on down through the ages until our very day. Remembering their lives and their example enlightens our own lives. Mentioning their names and asking for Allah's blessing on them in turn brings Divine blessing and favor on us.

May Allah bless an-Nabi (the Prophet) Muhammad (sas).

16   Links of Light: The Golden Chain

18 Links of Light: The Golden Chain

2
Abu Bakr as-Siddiq (ra)

After the death of the beloved Prophet (sas) his closest friend, Abu Bakr (ra), was chosen by Allah and the Companions to take his place as head of the community. On that sad day Abu Bakr (ra) remained as he always was, firm in his belief, steadfast in his service to the Prophet (sas) and Allah. When some of the Companions could not accept that the Prophet (sas) had actually died, thinking that such a man would live forever, Abu Bakr (ra) was the one to remind them that all of God's creatures must taste of death. Only Allah lives forever.

Abu Bakr (ra) took up the political duties of the Prophet (sas). He became the *Amir al-Mu'mineen*, the Commander of the Faithful, leader of the new Muslim state. He also shouldered the other main duty of the Prophet (sas), to serve as the spiritual guide of the Muslims. The Prophet (sas) had said, "All that Allah poured into my heart, I poured into the heart of Abu Bakr (ra)." The line of Prophets ended with Muhammad (sas). No more prophets were created to come after him until Sayyidina Mahdi (as) comes in the last days. Muhammad (sas) is called "the seal of the Prophets" because after his death the heavenly door through which prophecy enters this world was sealed shut. The new revelations of God's Book, the Quran, also ended. But the secret in the heart of the Prophet (sas) continued on in the heart of his inheritor, Abu Bakr (ra).

Abu Bakr (ra) was a wealthy merchant who knew and loved Muhammad (sas) even before the Quran began to be revealed. He was a quiet man, skilled in the poetic use of language and the interpretation of dreams. Although he was gentle he was also a warrior on the battlefield, and at all times a strong defender of what is right. As soon as he heard the first verses of God's Holy Book and the invitation of His Prophet (sas) he believed and accepted with all his heart. He was the first grown man to accept Islam.

Not only was Abu Bakr (ra) the first to accept but also he was, more importantly, the only one to accept without the least hesitation or doubt. The Prophet (sas) said that everyone to whom he spoke about the visits of Jibrail (as) and the Divine revelations showed at first some doubt that such an unusual and miraculous event could be real, everyone, that is, except Abu Bakr (ra). When the Prophet (sas) returned from the Night Journey through all the Heavens, everyone who heard the news felt a little doubt or disbelief, everyone, that is, except Abu Bakr (ra). For this reason the Prophet (sas) gave to him the title of *as-Siddiq*, meaning the one who witnesses the Truth. From that time on he was known as Abu Bakr as-Siddiq (ra). The Prophet (sas) knew that he could rely completely on Abu Bakr (ra) for support and assistance and that he would never fail him.

When the Prophet (sas) left Mecca for Medina he asked Abu Bakr (ra) to travel with him. In the dead of night they escaped those who wanted to murder them and fled into the mountains. They hid for three days in a cave on Mt. Thawr. They saw the dove build her nest and the tiny spider spin her web over the entrance to conceal their whereabouts. They heard their enemies searching and coming closer. They saw them actually peer into the cave through the unbroken web and yet see nothing within.

Protected by Allah, the Prophet (sas) and Abu Bakr (ra) took turns sleeping and keeping watch. At one point the Prophet (sas) laid his head on Abu Bakr's (ra) lap and fell asleep. A snake began to lift its head from a hole in the cave floor. Abu Bakr (ra) quickly stuffed his cloak into the hole. The snake appeared again from another hole and Abu Bakr (ra), having nothing left to block it and fearing that the snake would hurt his beloved Prophet (sas), placed the heel of his foot securely in the hole. The snake bit him hard and deep. Abu Bakr (ra) clenched his teeth so as not to move or cry out. He did not want to disturb the Prophet (sas). But a tear started in his eye from the pain and rolled down his cheek onto the face of the sleeping Prophet (sas). He woke immediately.

The snake then spoke in perfect Arabic, saying that all its life it had been waiting just to catch a glimpse of the Prophet (sas). It had meant no harm to either of them until Abu Bakr (ra) had prevented it from attaining its heart's desire, to gaze upon the face of the Prophet Muhammad (sas).

The Prophet (sas) greeted the snake and stroked its smooth back, forgiving and blessing it. He healed the foot of Abu Bakr (ra) and put his blessed hand on Abu Bakr's (ra) heart, that heart that steadfastly followed, protected and loved the Prophet (sas), that heart that put its own welfare second to that of its beloved, that heart that never turned or wavered in its devotion. He said, "All that Allah poured into my heart, I poured into the heart of Abu Bakr (ra)."

He told him that their seclusion in the cave was necessary, not just as a tactic to mislead their enemies but also, more importantly, as a time for a special spiritual event to take place. Then the Prophet (sas) ordered Abu Bakr (ra) to call the souls of the seven thousand and seven (7,007) saintly helpers who would succeed each other being born into the world until the end of time. Allah had given to His Prophet (sas) a light. The Prophet (sas) had placed that light into the heart of his inheritor, Abu Bakr as-Siddiq (ra) and now that light would be given in turn to each of the saints and shaykhs who would follow them down through the ages until the end of days.

The souls of these shaykhs appeared at the call of as-Siddiq (ra). Then they in turn called all the souls of the men and women who would follow and love them. Each follower put his right hand on the right shoulder of the person before him until they formed a line or chain. The final one put his hand on the hand of his Shaykh. Then Abu Bakr (ra) put his hand above the hands of all the Shaykhs and the Prophet (sas) put his hand above Abu Bakr's (ra). Above them all Allah rested His Hand of Power and He spoke with the Voice of Power. He told the Prophet (sas) to command Abu Bakr (ra) to order all the Prophets, Shaykhs and their followers to recite after Him,

Allahu Allahu Allahu Haqq
Allahu Allahu Allahu Haqq   Allah, Allah, Allah is Truth.
Allahu Allahu Allahu Haqq.

This was the first Dhikr.

Abu Bakr (ra) became the spiritual father of the shaykhs, saints, and their followers who took his hand in the cave. Just as a biological father is related to his children by the common blood that flows through their veins, so these souls are related to their spiritual father by the light of the secret that flows through their hearts. They are called the Golden Lineage or Chain, the Most Precious Family. Each Shaykh is a golden link in a line or chain that connects him to the Prophet (sas), link to link, heart to heart.

If we connect our heart to one of these Shaykhs, or links, we too will be safely anchored to the Prophet (sas) and his Way. Even if we do not see it, the secret of his great heart will begin to flow through us. And we will know that long before we were born into this world, our souls must have answered the call of Abu Bakr as-Siddiq (ra) and we were gathered in the presence of the Prophet (sas) in the cave on Thawr Mountain.

May Allah bless an-Nabi Muhammad (sas) and Abu Bakr as-Siddiq (ra).

24 Links of Light: The Golden Chain

3
Salman al-Farsi (ra)

Abu Bakr (ra) lived only two years before he followed his beloved Prophet (sas) into the unseen. Then the leadership of the Muslims was passed to Sayyidina Umar (ra) who became Commander of the Faithful. The secret of the heart passed from Abu Bakr (ra) to Salman al-Farsi (ra).

Salman (ra) came from a background that was completely different from the other Companions. He was not born an Arab but rather a Persian of the Zoroastrian religion. His father knew that Salman (ra) was special and kept him locked in the house in order to ensure his safety. One day the young Salman (ra) escaped his father's oppressive protection in order to explore his neighborhood. As he walked down the road he heard some Christians praying in a nearby church. His heart responded immediately. He stayed with the Christians and never returned home.

Salman (ra) became a servant to the wise old priest who taught him many things including that the next prophet was expected to appear in the near future in a village in Arabia. When the old priest died, Salman (ra) determined to make his way to Arabia to seek out this new prophet. On his journey he was captured by raiders and sold into slavery. Eventually he was bought by a man from one of the Jewish tribes living in the city of Medina. When he arrived there, Salman recognized the place from the descriptions of his Christian teacher. There he worked, tending to the date palms and orchards of his master. He wondered what Allah had in store for him. He began to hear talk about a man in Mecca who claimed to be a prophet, but Salman (ra) lived far from Mecca and could not get free to visit and see for himself.

One day, when Salman (ra) was high up in a palm tree harvesting dates, he saw

Muhammad (sas) and Abu Bakr (ra) arrive in Medina. He could see the glow of spiritual light around them. His heart longed to go immediately to greet them but he had to be patient for several months before he could leave his master's service even for a few hours. He found Muhammad (sas) sitting under a tree with his Companions. The old priest had told Salman (ra) the signs to look for in order to verify the identity of the Prophet (sas). Salman (ra) gave Muhammad (sas) some dates, saying they were given as charity (*sadaqa*). Muhammad (sas) passed them out to his Companions but touched none of them himself. Salman (ra) then gave Muhammad (sas) another handful of dates, saying they were being given as a personal gift to him. Muhammad (sas) thanked him kindly and ate from the dates with appreciation as well as sharing them with his Companions. This was just as the priest had said: the Prophet (sas) would never touch goods given as *sadaqa*, but he would receive with true thankfulness and pleasure any personal gift, however small.

Then Salman (ra) crept behind the Prophet (sas) in order to catch a glimpse of his back. The Prophet (sas), knowing what he wanted, let his robe slip off his shoulder. Between his blessed shoulder blades Salman (ra) saw the mark that is called the Seal of Prophecy. This mark had been made by the seal of a heavenly ring pressed onto Muhammad's (sas) back when he was just a baby. All the signs were fulfilled. Salman (ra) took the Prophet's (sas) hand and accepted Islam.

The Prophet (sas) himself raised the money to buy Salman (ra) from his master. He planted one hundred date palms with his own hands. By the blessing of his touch every single tree grew and produced fruit. The Prophet (sas) welcomed Salman (ra) into his own household where he was considered a member of the Prophet's (sas) family. The Prophet (sas) said, in reference to Salman (ra), "Even if true faith were to be placed up among the stars, people like Salman (ra) would find some way to reach it."

Salman (ra) lived with and served the Prophet (sas). It was his idea to dig the trench to protect Medina during what came to be known as the Battle of the Trench. This was the last battle between the Muslims of Medina and the unbelievers of Mecca. Because of his generosity and kindness to the poor, he came to be known as Salman the Good (ra). He had been educated by the Christian monks and could read the holy books of all the religions. He dedicated himself to memorizing and understanding the newest holy book, the Quran.

Salman (ra) led an ascetic and simple life. He clung strictly to the way of the Prophet (sas). He lived with very few material possessions, only what was absolutely necessary. Anything extra he gave to those he felt were more in need of them. He had only one cloak, which he wore during the day and used as a blanket at night. Like the Prophet (sas), he spent much of the night in prayer and the day in labor.

After the beloved Prophet's (sas) death, Salman (ra) continued to strictly follow his example. He joined the Muslim army until he stood with its commander, Saad ibn Abi Waqqas (ra), on the banks of the mighty Tigris River at the entrance to Persia. He prayed to Allah to make the crossing of rivers as easy for the desert Arabs as the crossing of sands. With that prayer, the two Companions plunged into the rough waters. The army followed until the river was literally covered with horses and men. It seemed that the horses were carried effortlessly on the waves until they reached the other side. Not a single man or horse was lost, only a small tin drinking cup. By his beautiful words and generous example he opened the hearts of the people of his homeland and gave them the precious gift of Islam. Sayyidina Umar (ra) appointed him governor over them. The large salary that was given to him by the state he gave away in charity. He continued to only eat food that he had worked for with his own hands.

He preferred to sleep outside rather than in a governor's mansion. In fact, he owned no house at all. One day a friend jokingly offered to build him a house that he would be sure to like. Salman (ra) was curious to know just what kind of house this could be. The man said, "I shall build you a house whose floor is so small that if you lie down your feet will hit the wall, and whose roof is so low that if you stand up you will bump your head."

Salman (ra) pursued closeness to Allah from his early childhood. He left his family and home in order to better serve his Lord. He traveled alone into unknown lands in his search for knowledge. He endured loss and hardship, poverty and slavery, without losing sight of his goal. When he attained that goal in finding the Prophet (sas), he put all he had at his service and in following his guidance. His heart was already open even before he met the Prophet (sas). It was open and ready to be filled with whatever the Prophet (sas) poured into it of his store of Divine Knowledge.

Before Abu Bakr (ra) passed away he poured his spiritual secrets and light into the heart of Salman (ra) who then became the guardian of the souls given in trust to the Prophet (sas). When Salman (ra) was getting ready to leave this world in 33 AH / 654 CE, he, in turn, poured this light into the heart of Sayyidina Qasim (ra), the grandson of Abu Bakr (ra).

May Allah bless an-Nabi Muhammad (sas), as-Siddiq (ra), and Salman (ra).

30 Links of Light: The Golden Chain

4
Qasim ibn Muhammad ibn Abu Bakr (ra)

Qasim (ra) was a brilliant beam of light that radiated from the most luminous spiritual family. His grandmother, Asma bint Umays (rah), was the sister of the Prophet's (sas) wife, Maymuna (rah). Asma (rah) was married to Jafar ibn Abi Talib (ra), the brother of Sayyidina Ali (ra). She and her husband left the persecution in Mecca, on the Prophet's (sas) orders, to find a safe haven in the Christian kingdom of Abyssinia. There they waited until the Prophet (sas) and the other Muslims would be able to join them. After ten years the Prophet (sas) asked them to return and join him in Medina. They had made two *hijras* (migrations) for Allah. They had left behind two homes, Mecca and Abyssinia, for His sake.

Not long after they returned, Jafar (ra) was killed in the battle of Muta'a. He carried the war banner of the Muslim army until his right arm was cut off. He then picked up the banner in his left hand until it also was severed. He died on the battlefield, a martyr. The Prophet (sas) said that he saw the angels taking Jafar (ra) to Paradise. Allah had replaced his two severed arms with beautiful wings. From then on he was remembered as Jafar at-Tayyar (ra), the flying Jafar (ra).

Some time later Asma (rah) married Abu Bakr as-Siddiq (ra). They had a son they named Muhammad ibn Abu Bakr (ra). Asma (rah) gave birth to him while accompanying the Prophet (sas) on his last pilgrimage to Mecca, called the Farewell Pilgrimage. The Prophet (sas) died and Abu Bakr (ra) followed him two years later. Asma (rah), widowed for the second time, married Sayyidina Ali (ra). It was considered a religious duty to marry the widows of fallen Muslims. In this way they were provided for and their children were raised with believing fathers. Sayyidina Ali (ra) raised Muhammad ibn Abu Bakr (ra) as a son and Muhammad (ra) grew to love Ali (ra) as a father. He fought beside him in all his battles.

When Ali (ra) became *Amir al-Mu'mineen*, leader of the Muslim state, he appointed Muhammad (ra) to be Governor of Egypt. There he was martyred, leaving his wife alone and pregnant. She returned to Medina and gave birth to a son she named Qasim ibn Muhammad ibn Abu Bakr (ra). After a while the boy went to live with his aunt, Aisha bint Abu Bakr (rah), who was a widow of the beloved Prophet (sas).

Sayyidatina Aisha (rah) had lived with the Prophet (sas) most of her life. She was one of the few to witness the visits of Jibrail (as) when he came to the Prophet (sas) to reveal sections of the Quran. On occasion Jibrail (as) even addressed Sayyidatina Aisha (rah) as well. She was very intelligent and remembered clearly in detail everything she heard. She memorized the whole Quran and after the death of the beloved Prophet (sas) her home became like a university. Men and women traveled from all over to hear her talk about the Prophet (sas) and recount his every word and deed. So Qasim (ra) was raised in her house, the heart of Islamic learning in Medina, and he became one of the seven most famous scholars of his day. All questions of religion eventually were brought to him to be debated and answered.

Imam Malik (q), upon whom the Maliki School of Islamic law is founded, said, "Qasim (ra) held in his heart the great secret and beautiful light that his grandfather, Abu Bakr (ra), had received from the Prophet (sas)."

Qasim (ra) continued to live in Medina and serve the Muslim community as a scholar and jurist. To those who came to him to learn more he gave the light from his heart. When he was getting older he had a vision in which his grandfather informed him that his days on this earth were coming to an end. Qasim (ra) asked for advice on how to die a good death. Abu Bakr (ra) replied, "Keep your tongue moist with the remembrance of Allah (*dhikr Allah*)." Qasim (ra) decided to make one last pilgrimage to Mecca just as the Prophet (sas) himself had done.

As he stood on Mount Arafat praying to Allah for the forgiveness of all mankind, he heard the mountain cry out in such a loud voice that all the startled pilgrims could hear. "Please, O Qasim," it cried, "please don't forget to pray for me also on the Day of Judgement."

Qasim (ra) returned to Mecca in order to circle God's House, the Ka'aba, seven times to complete his hajj and to say goodbye. This is called the "farewell *tawwaf*." He found the Ka'aba with a stream of water flowing out of its great doors and flooding the sacred enclosure. The Ka'aba was crying because this was the last time it would be together with Qasim (ra) in this world. It is said that the Ka'aba then picked itself up and made seven circles around Qasim (ra) as a farewell *tawwaf* to him.

Qasim (ra) died on his way home to Medina in 109 AH / 726 CE. Before he died he poured the light of his heart into the heart of his grandson, Jafar as-Sadiq (q).

May Allah bless an-Nabi (sas), as-Siddiq (ra), Salman (ra), and Qasim (ra).

34   Links of Light: The Golden Chain

5

Jafar as-Sadiq (ra)

Jafar (ra) was born in the beginning of the month of Ramadan in 83 AH / 702 CE. His mother was the daughter of Qasim (ra) and his father was Muhammad al-Baqir (ra), who was the son of Zain al-Abidin (ra), who was the son of Husayn (ra), who was the son of Sayyidina Ali (ra) and Sayyidatina Fatima (rah), daughter of the Prophet (sas). Therefore, on his father's side he descended from Ali (ra) and the Prophet (sas) and on his mother's side he was a great grandson of Abu Bakr as-Siddiq (ra). The rivers that welled up from these two main sources of secret knowledge came together and pooled in the heart of Jafar as-Sadiq (ra). From his heart the light of the Prophet (sas) radiated out to all mankind.

Jafar (ra) spent his life teaching others. In every word and deed he served as an example of the way of the Prophet (sas). He lived simply and rejected all honors and positions of power, although many were offered him. He upheld the law of the Quran but always with mercy and tolerance. He was a light and a guide to all around him and there is no one in the whole Muslim world, whatever their other differences, who does not love and respect him, even to this day.

Imam at-Tabari (q) related a story that he heard about Jafar (ra). In 113 AH / 731 CE a man called Layth ibn Saad went to Mecca to perform the pilgrimage. After the noon prayer Layth stayed in the mosque to read Quran. He began to hear the man next to him making dhikr. First the man said, "Ya Allah." He said it over and over until he had no more breath to say it any more. Then he began to say, "Ya Hayy" (O Source of Life), until his voice became hoarse and his breath was gone. Then, in a whisper, he asked, "O Allah, I would like to soothe my throat with some of Your sweet grapes. Please give me some. Also, my Lord, since my robe is so worn out and full of holes that it barely covers me, please give me a new robe."

Layth went on to say that hardly had this unknown man finished his unusual prayer when a bowl of juicy grapes and two robes of the best quality and most beautiful design appeared beside him. Layth said to the man, "O my partner, please share these gifts with me." The man asked Layth, "In what way are you my partner?" Layth replied, "When you prayed asking for them I said, 'Amin.'" (It is the custom when a request is made out loud, asking Allah for His favors, that those who are nearby support the request by saying "Amin".) The man smiled at that. "Come then," he said. "Eat with me and dress yourself with the robe of your choice." They sat together for a while, sharing the gift of grapes in silence. Then the unknown man said goodbye and left the mosque.

Layth followed the man outside and saw a beggar in ragged clothes approach him and ask for something. The unknown man immediately gave the beggar the second robe. Layth tried to follow further but the man disappeared from sight. Layth asked the beggar if he happened to know the name of the one who had most generously given him the robe. The beggar replied that the mysterious man was the famous scholar and grandson of the Prophet (sas), Jafar as-Sadiq (ra).

Jafar (ra) understood truly that all things come only from Allah and return only to Him. Therefore, when he had need of anything, however small, the only one he asked for help was Allah Almighty Himself. Other people could get what they needed by asking from Jafar (ra).

Jafar (ra) died in Medina at 75 years of age and was buried near his most beloved ancestors. Before he died he safeguarded the secret of his heart to be poured later into the heart of Tayfur Abu Yazid al-Bistami (q) who was still waiting to be born.

May Allah bless an-Nabi (sas), as-Siddiq (ra), Salman (ra), Qasim (ra), and Jafar (ra).

38 Links of Light: The Golden Chain

6

Tayfur Abu Yazid al-Bistami (q)

Tayfur Abu Yazid (q) was born in about 188 AH / 800 CE in Bistam in northeastern Persia. His grandfather, like Salman's (ra) father, was a follower of the Zoroastrian religion, who worshipped fire. His father converted to Islam and married a very spiritual woman. She knew, even while she was pregnant, that she was carrying a special soul. Every time she tried to eat a piece of food grown or cooked by a person whose heart did not accept Allah, the baby kicked and squirmed until she spit out the food. Throughout his life Tayfur Abu Yazid (q) was very careful about all the food he ate. He made sure it was produced and cooked by a believing hand and bought with money earned in a legal way.

As a young child Tayfur's (q) mother sent him to school to study the Quran. One day he began to read the passage in *Sura Luqman* that says, "Be thankful to Me (Allah) and to your parents" (31:14). Tayfur (q) quickly excused himself from class and ran home to his mother, very upset. He told her that his heart was not able to serve two masters. Either he must serve his mother completely or she must free him to serve Allah completely. His mother released him from his obligations to her and told him, "Go and be God's."

Tayfur Abu Yazid (q) left Bistam to travel the world in search of wisdom. He studied with one hundred and thirteen (113) shaykhs and took benefit from all of them. He traveled the path of self-denial and physical hardship. He ate little and fasted much. He slept rarely and prayed constantly. After seventeen years he determined to make the pilgrimage to Allah's

Holy House in Mecca. He traveled slowly on foot. Any time, in any village or town through which he passed, if there was a mosque, large or small, he stopped to pray and meditate. In this way it took him twelve full years to reach Mecca. After spending a year in Mecca he set out to visit the Prophet's (sas) grave in Medina. The light that glowed within him began to be visible and to attract others. A lot of people wanted to join him on his journey. Because he was afraid that they would be thinking of him rather than of their Lord or their Prophet (sas), he turned to the crowd and declared, "I am God. There is no God but me. Worship me." At the time he said this he was in a spiritual state of oneness with Allah. There was an actual truth in what he said but the people could not understand this so they scattered in horror. Tayfur (q) entered Medina alone and at peace.

While he was praying at the Prophet's (sas) tomb he received news that his mother was not well. He was ordered by Allah to return to Bistam. The news of his saintliness traveled ahead of him. When he entered Bistam throngs of admiring people were there to greet him. It was the fasting month of Ramadan. He pulled out a loaf of bread and began to eat. The crowd was horrified by this display and quickly scurried away in disgust. Tayfur (q), in contentment, said, "I obeyed the sacred law and all people rejected me." Allah says in the Holy Quran that a man who is traveling long distances during Ramadan may put off his fast until he comes to the end of his journey. He must make up the fasting days he missed at another time, whenever he is able. The crowd, in its ignorance, misjudged Tayfur Abu Yazid (q).

Tayfur (q) came to his mother's house alone. Through the closed door he heard her praying to Allah to watch over her dear son in whatever distant land he might be. Tears welled up in his eyes as he knocked at her door. His mother opened it and could hardly believe her eyes. It had been thirty years since he had left and all that time she had been praying for his safe return. She was overwhelmed with joy.

That night, after she had already gotten in bed, his mother asked Tayfur (q) to bring her a cup of water. He went to the pitcher, but it was empty. He went to the large jar in which they stored water and found it empty also. He picked up the pitcher and went out into the freezing night and down the steep icy path to the river. There he broke the ice and filled the pitcher with water. When he returned he found that his mother had already fallen back asleep. He waited by her door, standing in the cold darkness until the handle of the pitcher froze to his fingers. He feared she would wake and he would not hear her. Finally she woke and drank a little water. When she saw his condition she cried, asking God to bless him. She told him to put down the pitcher and rest. If he left her door ajar he would be sure to hear her if she called.

For the rest of that night Tayfur Abu Yazid (q) lay awake, worrying that his mother's door would blow closed in the chill draft, or that he would sleep so soundly he would not hear her call to him. Then at dawn, he later related, all that he had been searching for in his thirty years of study and travel, self-discipline and worship, slipped in gently through his mother's open door. What he thought to be the less important service turned out to be the greater. For serving his mother with love Allah rewarded Tayfur (q) with a journey through the seven Heavens in the blessed footsteps of our beloved Prophet Muhammad (sas). And his heart opened to receive the secrets that Jafar (ra) had put in safekeeping for him. Tayfur Abu Yazid (q) is *Uwaysi* because his heart connected directly to the heart of the Shaykh without ever having met him in person.

Tayfur (q) then settled down in Bistam and began to gather around him those who were looking for a way to get closer to God. One of his students said that he often prayed the noon prayer behind the Shaykh. When Tayfur Abu Yazid (q) raised his hands to begin the prayer he could hardly say the words "Allahu Akbar" because his fear and respect for Allah were so great. His whole body would begin to shake and tremble. The effort to overcome his awe was so intense that the student could hear terrible sounds, as if all the bones in Tayfur's (q) body were being crushed.

One day as he was walking, a dirty stray dog brushed past him. Tayfur Abu Yazid (q) quickly gathered his robe around him and stepped out of its way. Allah gave the dog human speech and it moaned miserably because this great saint had shunned it. Tayfur (q) immediately recognized that this was a lesson from Allah and he was ashamed. Although he was a great saint and a scholar he was not too proud to accept a dog as a teacher. He asked the dog's pardon. The dog was only unclean on the outside but Tayfur (q) must be unclean on the inside to think he was worthy of more respect than any other of God's creatures.

The dog continued howling in order to explain in what ways it was worthy of the Saint's respect. Wherever it went men threw stones at it and chased it away, while they treated Tayfur (q) as if he were a king. In reality we are all servants. Only Allah is King. The dog owned nothing, no clothes nor stores of food. It relied totally on Allah to provide for it every day. Tayfur (q), on the other hand, was at that moment in possession of many things including enough food to last for at least a month. Tayfur Abu Yazid (q) sat down in the dusty road and now it was his turn to cry. "I am not even good enough to travel with a dog," he sighed. Then he raised his hands to heaven and thanked the All-Mercifull Lord, Who is able to guide even the highest of His creations by means of the humblest.

Tayfur Abu Yazid (q) died in Bistam and was buried there but he passed on his secret and his light to Abul Hasan al-Kharqani (q).

May Allah bless an-Nabi (sas), as-Siddiq (ra), Salman (ra), Qasim (ra), Jafar (ra), and Tayfur (q).

Tayfur Abu Yazid al-Bistami (q) 43

44 Links of Light: The Golden Chain

7
Abul Hasan al-Kharqani (q)

During his last years, every time Abu Yazid (q) passed through the town of Kharqan, a suburb of Bistam, he would marvel at the wonderful perfume which it seemed only he could smell there. He told his students that a child was going to be born in Kharqan who would be a great saint and who would grow up to be his inheritor. Indeed thirty-nine (39) years after the death of Tayfur Abu Yazid (q), a boy was born in the town of Kharqan. He was known as Abul Hasan (q). Even as a young boy it was his practice to go alone to the grave of Tayfur (q) to pray and meditate. Abul Hasan (q) used to say that to the world Tayfur (q) was considered dead but to him Tayfur Abu Yazid (q) was very much alive and his dearest companion. One night, after many years of teaching and watching him, Tayfur (q) poured into the heart of Abul Hasan (q) all his heavenly secrets and the light that had been handed down from the Prophet (sas). Abul Hasan (q), in the tradition of Uways al-Qarni (ra), was given his secret from the unseen and because of this he was called *Uwaysi*.

After that night all kinds of spiritual powers began to appear in Abul Hasan (q). He could now both read and recite all of the Holy Quran, whereas before he was hardly able to distinguish one letter from another. A student came to him asking to study hadith, the sayings and doings of the Prophet Muhammad (sas) as recorded by those who knew him. As the student read each hadith, Abul Hasan (q) would tell him simply if it was correct or not. After some time the student challenged Abul Hasan (q) to tell him how he knew if the hadith was right or wrong. Abul Hasan (q) answered that since the Prophet (sas) stood before his eyes at all times, if something incorrect was read, Abul Hasan (q) could tell immediately by the slight frown that appeared on the Prophet's (sas) noble face.

Abul Hasan (q) made his living as a farmer. His house was a humble cottage. When he hoed the stony ground to plant his crops Allah would cause gold and diamonds to sparkle in the turned earth. Abul Hasan (q) would quickly bury them back into the ground because he did not want to take any chance that worldly riches would entice him away from his complete reliance on Allah.

One day the Sultan of that region, Mahmud Ghazni, decided to pay a visit to Abul Hasan (q). The Sultan thought it would be amusing to trade clothes with his servant and so he entered the humble house of the Shaykh in disguise. But Abul Hasan (q) was not fooled. He did not stand to greet either of his guests and he persisted in talking only to Mahmud, even though he was dressed as the servant. When he was leaving Sultan Mahmud thanked Abul Hasan (q) and, as he looked around him, the humble cottage of the Shaykh looked very beautiful and peaceful. Abul Hasan (q) frowned and scolded the Sultan, "O you, to whom Allah has given a vast kingdom, do you now wish to have my simple cottage as well?" Sultan Mahmud turned bright red in shame for his envious thoughts. Then the Shaykh rose to his feet for the first time and escorted the Sultan respectfully to the door.

The embarrassed Sultan asked why Abul Hasan (q) had stood up now and not when he had first entered. The Shaykh answered that when Mahmud had arrived, even though dressed as a servant, he had been wrapped in his kingly pride. Now, however, with the color of humility clearly visible on his face, the Shaykh rose to honor him for being a humble servant of the only true Sultan, Allah.

Abul Hasan (q) then gave Sultan Mahmud a piece of his cloak as a parting gift. The Sultan kept it with him always. One day, when the Sultan was far away fighting in India, he realized that his soldiers were losing the battle. He took Abul Hasan's (q) gift in his hands and asked Allah, for the sake of His servant Abul Hasan (q), to bring success to the Sultan's armies. The tide of the battle turned and victory was won.

That night Sultan Mahmud had a dream in which Abul Hasan (q) scolded him for wasting his precious prayer on a battle. If he had instead asked for the whole world to become believers and live in peace Allah would have granted it. Such was the power of asking in the name of the Saint.

Abul Hasan (q) lived simply and was very hard on his self in order to bring his ego under his control. For forty years he craved a cool drink of water and for forty years Abul Hasan (q) refused himself the pleasure. He fasted most days and stayed awake praying most nights, until he had no thirst, no hunger and no need for sleep. He used to say that when he felt hungry a delicious sweet substance would appear in his stomach by God's order. He had no need for other food. Allah provided his food, his drink, and his only companionship. He wanted nothing but to be left alone by the world to keep the company of his Lord.

Allah, however, had other wishes and He directed Abul Hasan (q) to build a center and teach those who came to him. Allah made the Shaykh as a mercy for all people. By sitting with Abul Hasan (q) those who searched for God would find Him. Those who even think about Abul Hasan (q) or mention his name will gain great spiritual benefit.

Abul Hasan (q) died in Kharqan and was buried near Tayfur Abu Yazid (q). He passed his secrets and his light to Abu Ali al-Farmadi (q).

May Allah bless an-Nabi (sas), as-Siddiq (ra), Salman (ra), Qasim (ra), Jafar (ra), Tayfur (q), and Abul Hasan (q).

8
Abu Ali al-Farmadi (q)

Abu Ali (q) was born in Khurasan in about 392 AH / 1,000 CE. He lived and died in the village of Farmad on the outskirts of the city of Tus.

Different from the shaykhs immediately preceding him, Abu Ali (q) was trained as a religious scholar, educated in all the Islamic sciences. He studied law according to the Shafi School with the most famous scholars of his time. They called him "The Tongue of Khurasan" because when he began to give lectures they were brilliant with the light of heavenly knowledge. It was said that when people gathered around him the gathering became like a garden full of flowers. Those who listened to him found their hearts opening like roses in the light of the sun. He had a special way about him that caused hearts to fill with joy and contentment in his company.

He studied under some of the most renowned and respected scholars of his day. Among them was al-Ghazali al-Kabir (q), the father of Abdul Hamid al-Ghazali (q), known as "The Proof of Islam". Al-Ghazali al-Kabir (q) said that he had never encountered anyone quite like Abu Ali (q). He had a way of talking and teaching that was both delicate and beautiful. His manner of treating all people was gentle and considerate. He made them feel at ease and drawn to remember Allah. He was an example of kindness and good conduct. Although he was famous and had many scholarly degrees he behaved humbly and thoughtfully towards everyone. He was both a scholar and a gentleman.

Abu Ali (q), however, was not content with just learning from books. He wanted a guide who could teach him the secrets that can only be passed from one heart to another. He was drawn to the Shaykhs on the path of remembrance (dhikr), and he treated them above all with respect and humility. He advised all his students to follow this way if they wanted success.

One day he accompanied his Shaykh to the public bath. In the eleventh century people did not have showers or bathtubs in their houses. The government built public bathhouses where water was heated in large pools and the steam collected under high domed ceilings. Here people of the town would come at least once a week before the Friday prayers to soak and scrub and steam themselves until every pore was clean and warm. In the steamy heat of the bath they would occasionally pour cold well water over themselves to refresh them in the heat and to increase blood flow. Abu Ali (q) stood respectfully beside the door while his Shaykh entered. Even though he was a famous scholar and master of law his true pleasure was in spending time in the company of his Shaykh and being of help to him, in any way possible.

Abu Ali (q) went out into the snow and drew a bucket of cold water from the well. Without looking he set it carefully, attracting no attention, inside the door of the steamy bath and returned to stand outside. After his bath the Shaykh came out and asked who had provided the bucket of cold water. Abu Ali (q) looked down at his feet and said nothing. He was terrified that he had committed an act of disrespect or done something wrong. Three times his Shaykh asked who was responsible for putting the bucket of cold water inside the bathhouse. The third time Abu Ali (q) raised his head and quietly admitted that he was responsible. His Shaykh looked him in the eyes and in that one look poured all the heavenly knowledge that he had acquired through seventy years of hard struggle, into the heart of Abu Ali (q). For the humble service and thoughtfulness of that one bucket of water Abu Ali (q) received a heart full of the knowledge of God.

All his life Abu Ali (q) advised his followers that if they wanted to be successful they must love their Shaykh above all else and be respectful towards him. He advised them to avoid the company of the rich and powerful whose manner of living might distract them from their Shaykh. He continued that they should turn their eyes away from the society and daily activities of the average people also, for that too might distract them from their

Shaykh. They should focus on the face of the Shaykh just as the Companions focused on the face of the Prophet (sas). The Blessed Prophet (sas) said, "Whoever sees the face of one who knows God, sees me," and "Whoever sees me has seen the Truth."

Abu Ali (q) died in 477 AH / 1084 CE and was buried in his hometown of Farmad in what is now Iran. All Abu Ali (q) had inherited he poured into the heart of Abu Ya'qub Yusuf al-Hamadani (q).

May Allah bless an-Nabi (sas), as-Siddiq (ra), Salman (ra), Qasim (ra), Jafar (ra), Tayfur (q), Abul Hasan (q), and Abu Ali (q).

52 Links of Light: The Golden Chain

9
Abu Ya'qub Yusuf al-Hamadani (q)

Born in 440 AH/1048 CE in Hamadan, Shaykh Yusuf (q) moved to Baghdad when he was eighteen. Baghdad was the center of learning and the political capital of the Muslim world at that time. There he went to the Islamic University and studied under the greatest shaykhs and scholars of his day, attaining universal recognition for his brilliance and ability. But the light in his heart was given to him by Abu Ali al-Farmadi (q).

Shaykh Yusuf (q) is reported to have been tall and thin with brown skin and a face scarred by childhood illness. He wore woolen clothing, even in summer, that he patched himself when it became threadbare. Under all circumstances people found him to be cheerful and kind. Whatever wealth was given to him he passed on to those in need. He never kept anything for himself. Wherever he was, whatever else he was doing, he continued to make dhikr and recite Quran on each breath. It is said that he had in his keeping the walking stick and the turban of Salman al-Farsi (ra). He was given by Allah the remarkable ability to be able to appear and disappear whenever he liked.

His reputation as a scholar and a holy man spread throughout the Muslim world. Three young friends, who were already recognized scholars, decided to travel to Baghdad to visit the famous Shaykh Yusuf (q). The first was Abu Said who wanted to ask the Shaykh to clarify a question of Islamic law. The second was Ibn Saqa who wanted to test the Shaykh by trying to ask a question to which he would have no answer. The third was Abdul Qadir al-Jilani (q) who simply wanted to pay his respects to a man of God and receive his blessing.

The three friends entered the mosque of Shaykh Yusuf (q) but did not see him. The Shaykh was present but he veiled himself from their sight so that he could observe them. After some time he appeared to them. They had had no time to introduce themselves but Shaykh Yusuf (q) addressed them each by name. First he said, "O Ibn Saqa, how dare you ask me a question only to try and outwit me. I know your question and here is its answer. I see the fire of unbelief burning in your heart."

Then Shaykh Yusuf (q) turned to Abu Said and answered his, as yet unasked, question. He scolded him for his lack of respect in coming to greet the Shaykh with the sole purpose of gaining useless information. But he blessed his intention, which was to seek knowledge, and predicted that Abu Said would achieve worldly success as a lawyer and a scholar.

Finally, he turned to Abdul Qadir (q) and asked him to step closer to receive his blessing. Then Shaykh Yusuf (q) poured into his open heart heavenly secrets and predicted that one day Abdul Qadir (q) would attain such a spiritual level that all the other saints would bow down before him.

All that Shaykh Yusuf (q) predicted came to pass. Abu Said became a successful lawyer, famous and wealthy. Abdul Qadir al-Jilani (q) became one of the most well known saints, whose spiritual path is still followed to this day. As for Ibn Saqa, his story is quite sad.

Because of his talent for argument the Sultan sent Ibn Saqa to debate the Christian scholars in the Byzantine capital of Constantinople. In the debate he proved invincible. The Byzantine emperor was so impressed that he invited Ibn Saqa to dine with the royal family. At that dinner Ibn Saqa fell madly in love with the Emperor's daughter. She consented to marry him only on the condition that he leave Islam and become a Christian. He converted and married the princess.

After this Ibn Saqa slid slowly into madness. All the light left his face and the princess divorced him. He began to wander the streets, homeless and begging for food. Abu Said went to try to rescue his friend. He found him dying, dirty and crazy in the alleys of Constantinople. Ibn Saqa, who had memorized the whole of the Quran and all the law books, could barely remember anything. With his dying breath the only passage of the Quran that he could recall was the verse that reads, "Again and again will those who disbelieve wish that they were Muslims" (15:2). No matter how often Abu Said turned his friend's face towards Mecca, Ibn Saqa turned his face away.

Because the Shaykh is the representative of the Prophet (sas) your attitude towards him is important. Respect, or lack of it, has consequences in this world and the next. Abdul Qadir (q) came to the Shaykh with an open heart, as a humble servant. Into his open heart Shaykh Yusuf (q) poured Divine Secrets. Abu Said came with an open mind, asking for intellectual knowledge. Into his open mind Shaykh Yusuf (q) poured Islamic knowledge. But Ibn Saqa came with a closed heart and a closed mind. He thought he already knew everything worth knowing. Into his heart and mind Shaykh Yusuf (q) could find no room to pour anything at all. He was left without blessing to fall into the terrible hole he had dug for himself. Even the Prophet (sas) used to pray Allah not to leave him without Divine Guidance even for the blink of an eye.

Shaykh Yusuf (q) returned to his homeland later in life. He settled in Merv and built a school and a mosque where he taught the many students who were attracted to him. After years of teaching he went into seclusion to pray and meditate in solitude. He died in Khurasan on the twelfth of *Rabia al-Awwal*, 535 AH / 1140 CE. He poured the secrets of his heart into the heart of Abul Abbas al-Khidr (as) to be held in trust for Abdul Khaliq al-Ghujdawani (q).

May Allah bless an-Nabi (sas), as-Siddiq (ra), Salman (ra), Qasim (ra), Jafar (ra), Tayfur (q), Abul Hasan (q), Abu Ali (q), and Yusuf (q).

10
Abul Abbas al-Khidr (as)

Some say he is a prophet. Some say he is a saint. Sayyidina Khidr (as) is, however, most definitely a mysterious figure. No one knows when he was born or where. Four prophets known to us have yet to die. Two were taken still alive straight into Heaven, Idris (as) and Isa (as). Two, however, remain on the earth helping people and teaching them. Ilyas (as) helps those on the sea and Khidr (as) helps those on the land. The name, "Khidr," literally means, "the green one." The Prophet Muhammad (sas) told his Companions that wherever Khidr (as) steps, the dry earth becomes green and living. Khidr (as) is also known as "the Ancient One" because stories of him can be found in all traditions going back thousands of years.

The most well known story of Khidr (as) is found in *Surat al-Kahf* in the Holy Quran. It is said that the great prophet Musa (as) was ordered by Allah to find a teacher. All men, no matter how enlightened they may already be, sometimes need a guide and a teacher. Musa (as) was told to walk alongside the river until the dry, dead fish in his lunch basket became alive and jumped into the water and swam away. At that point he would know that his teacher, Sayyidina Khidr (as), was near.

Khidr (as) was not happy to take on Musa (as) as his student. He told him repeatedly that he would not be able to follow or understand. But Musa (as) insisted, so Khidr (as) permitted him to accompany him on the condition that he not question or object to anything he saw.

Khidr (as) decided to cross the river. A fisherman offered to take them on his boat for no charge. When they reached the other side and the fisherman unloaded his catch and went home, Khidr (as) chopped a big hole in the side of the boat. Musa (as) was horrified and let Khidr (as) know how he felt. Khidr (as) reminded him of his promise not to question anything he saw. Musa (as) became silent and determined to try harder to follow his teacher.

Walking down the road, they came across a young boy playing. Khidr (as) pointed to the boy and he immediately fell down dead. Without looking back Khidr (as) continued on his way. Now Musa (as) was really upset. What could possibly justify killing an innocent child? Again he questioned his teacher until Khidr (as) silenced him by reminding him again of his promise.

They entered a village for the night and asked for food and shelter. The villagers were most inhospitable and refused them anything. Khidr (as) and Musa (as) spent the night huddled against a crumbling wall, hungry and tired. In the morning Khidr (as) began to repair the stone wall so that it would not fall down. Musa (as) lost patience again. Sore, after a night on the hard ground, and hungry, he protested. Why should they work for free for the benefit of people who had not even offered them a drink of water? If they were going to work they should at least have asked to be paid for it.

Forgetting his promise for the third time, Musa (as) realized that he could not follow Sayyidina Khidr (as). Before they parted company, Khidr (as) insisted that they share a meal after which he would explain the reasons behind all that Musa (as) had thought he had seen.

Some say that at that time a small deer passed by. Khidr (as) pointed at her with his finger and the deer fell down dead. When they went up to her they found one half of her body was roasted and ready to eat, while the other half was still raw. Khidr (as) said the uncooked half belonged to Musa (as) because he had asked for payment for his work and so Allah had paid him. The cooked half belonged to Khidr (as) because he was content to accept from Allah whatever gift He chose to give. While Musa (as) collected firewood and cooked his meat, Khidr (as) explained to him the hidden meanings behind the events of the previous day.

He had chopped a hole in the boat of the generous fisherman because a tyrant was on his way to collect all the sea-worthy boats for use in transporting his army. If the boat looked to be in need of repair it would not be seized.

He had killed the young boy because his character was weak and he would grow up to be a liar and an unbeliever. The parents of the boy were good people and would suffer much from the boy's actions. Allah intended to send them another child, a daughter so strong and good that she would be grandmother to many saints.

As for the broken wall, under it was buried a treasure that belonged rightfully to two orphan boys. If the wall should fall, the greedy villagers would find the treasure and steal it before the boys were old enough to protect themselves. By repairing the wall Khidr (as) ensured that the treasure would remain hidden until the boys came of age to claim it. Their grandfather had been a saint and their father a pious man. Allah protects His friends and their families. All that Khidr (as) had done had been according to the Will of Allah.

Then Khidr (as) picked up the skin of the little deer they had eaten for lunch. In his hands she became warm and alive and she bounded away into the bushes. The Prophet Muhammad (sas) told his Companions that he wished that Musa (as) had been able to be more patient. If he had, we would all have learned more wisdom from Khidr (as).

No matter how smart you are or how many favors Allah has given you there is always someone who knows more or is more favored. Like plates stacked one upon the other, the Quran says, there is always someone above you and also someone below you. We have no idea how tall the stack or where our position is within it. But we are, each and every one of us, a necessary part of the whole. In front of the vast and infinite wonders of Allah we must all be humble. Every one at some time has need of someone to guide him. Even the Prophet Muhammad (sas) took the Archangel Jibrail (as) as his guide.

The Prophet (sas) himself met Khidr (as) who visited him at least once to declare his Islam and be taught the secrets of *Surat al-Fatihah*. At the time of the Prophet's (sas) death his Companions entered the small room, where he was lying, to say their farewells. Some of them heard from the corner of the crowded room a voice giving greetings of peace and blessing the family of the Prophet (sas). This they recognized later, as the voice of Khidr (as).

Khidr (as) continues to guide people to this day. When he is remembered or his name is mentioned, he appears, whether you can see him or not. He may appear as an ordinary person of any age except that the look in his eye might catch your attention and maybe his coat will blow open just enough to reveal a flash of shimmering green.

Shaykh Yusuf al-Hamadani (q) asked Khidr (as) to hold the secret in trust and to train his successor, Abdul Khaliq (q), until he was ready to receive the secret into his own heart.

May Allah bless an-Nabi (sas), as-Siddiq (ra), Salman (ra), Qasim (ra), Jafar (ra), Tayfur (q), Abul Hasan (q), Abu Ali (q), Yusuf (q), and Abul Abbas al-Khidr (as).

64 Links of Light: The Golden Chain

11
Abdul Khaliq al-Ghujdawani (q)

In Malatya, in eastern Turkey, there lived a man, respected as a scholar and as a spiritual teacher, whose name was Abdul Jamil (q). He was called Imam Abdul Jamil (q) because he was a descendant of Imam Malik, the founder of the Maliki School of Islamic Law. It is said that one of his intimate companions was Abul Abbas al-Khidr (as). As a young man he was inspired to move to what is now Uzbekistan. There he married a princess, the daughter of the Seljuk ruler of Bukhara. They had a son who, on the advice of Khidr (as), they named Abdul Khaliq (q), meaning servant of the Creator.

Abdul Khaliq (q) grew up in Ghujdawan on the outskirts of Bukhara. He studied Arabic and the Islamic Sciences with his father and the spiritual realities with his father's friend, Abul Abbas al-Khidr (as). Khidr (as) took him on many miraculous journeys and introduced him to prophets and saints both living and dead. When he was twenty-two Khidr (as) took him to meet Yusuf al-Hamadani (q). From that day until Shaykh Yusuf's (q) death, Abdul Khaliq (q) stayed in his company and served him with all his heart.

Shaykh Yusuf (q) taught him his practice of reciting dhikr on each breath. One day as he was studying Quran a line that he had read many times before suddenly caught his attention. That line read, "Call on your Lord in humbleness and in secrecy..." (7:55). Allah inspired Abdul Khaliq (q) by means of this *ayat* and he conceived a desire to learn the way of the secret remembrance, or dhikr, mentioned in this verse.

For many years Abdul Khaliq (q) prayed to Allah to teach him the secret dhikr that he had read about in the Quran. Finally Allah fulfilled his wish by ordering Khidr (as) to teach him. Khidr (as) told Abdul Khaliq (q) to go to the river and submerge himself in its waters. Here, surrounded by water, (which Shaytan cannot penetrate because he is made of fire), without the distraction of his breath going in and out, in complete isolation, he would learn the secret dhikr of the heart. Everyday Abdul Khaliq (q) would practice this exercise until he could stay submerged for long periods of time. Finally his heart opened and he found what he had been searching for. Then Khidr (as) poured into his open heart all the lights and secrets inherited from the Prophet (sas) that Shaykh Yusuf (q) had given Khidr (as) to hold in trust for him.

Abdul Khaliq (q) expressed in eight concise phrases the design and principles of his Way that later came to be called the Naqshbandi Way. These phrases may seem simple but they have many levels of meaning and whole books have been written trying to explain them.

The Eight Principles of the Naqshbandi Way are:

1. Mindful Breathing. Watch your breath. Become aware of the automatic action, in and out, of your breathing. By concentrating on this, all other things will be forgotten.
2. Watch your Step. During the day keep your eyes focused on your feet. You will be less likely to make a misstep and will not get distracted by the purposeless activity around you.
3. Journey Homeward. Search for what is best in the world around you. Look for a teacher and when you find him stay with him. Continue the journey inwardly, always traveling from what is good to what is better.
4. Solitude in the Crowd. Be alone even while keeping company with people. Keep your heart and mind safely wrapped in a state of awareness of God even while you continue to interact normally with people.
5. Remembrance. Remember Allah at all times by doing dhikr on each breath, "La ilaha illa Allah".
6. Returning. Realize that you came from Allah and you are always traveling towards Him. Allah is your only goal. When you achieve this state wherever you look you will see only Allah.

7. <u>Attentiveness</u>. Expel from your heart all useless thoughts or bad desires. If you can keep this awareness and purity for even fifteen minutes you have achieved much.
8. <u>Recollection</u>. Expel from your heart not only the bad but also all things, bad or good, other than Allah Almighty. Keep your mind and heart continually in the Divine Presence. If you can do this, all that you think, see, or feel, is Truth.

These principles should serve, at the very least, to increase our humility and our understanding that the reality of the saints who have achieved them is altogether different from our own. We need to respect these saints, love them, and help them however we can.

Abdul Khaliq (q) wrote a letter to his son that has become very famous because it expresses in a short and simple way the great saint's recipe for proper living. He wrote:

"Follow in the Way of the Prophet (sas) and his Companions (rahum) by studying the Quran and Hadith. Keep company with sincere believers and avoid ignorant people. Pray in congregation whenever possible but do not be the leader. Beware of fame and avoid the company of the rich and famous. Talk little, eat little, sleep little and run from social gatherings as you would run from a lion. Eat lawful food and leave anything that makes you doubt.

"Do not laugh too much because that will deaden the heart. Do not tease or humiliate anyone, or praise yourself. Do not argue. Do not ask anyone, except God, for anything and do not become a burden on others. Do not ask others to serve you but serve others. Do not criticize your teachers because they know more than you.

"Make each of your actions sincere by intending them only to please Allah. Pray to Him in humbleness. Let your business be righteousness, the mosque be your home and let your friend be your Lord."

Abdul Khaliq (q) was a living example of these principles. He established a school and mosque near his hometown on the outskirts of Bukhara, where people from all over the world came to worship and study. Even the Ka'aba honored Abdul Khaliq (q). When it was refitted with new doors the old doors, which had been touched lovingly by so many worshippers for so many years, flew from the Holy House in Mecca to Abdul Khaliq's (q) side in Bukhara. They can still be seen to this day by his grave. He died in 575 AH / 1179 CE. Nearby lies a well whose waters, because of Abdul Khaliq's (q) blessing, heal the sick.

Today there are still hundreds of people who come each day to drink and pray and pay their respects.

Abdul Khaliq (q) poured the light in his heart into the heart of his student and successor, Arif ar-Rivgari (q).

May Allah bless an-Nabi (sas), as-Siddiq (ra), Salman (ra), Qasim (ra), Jafar (ra), Tayfur (q), Abul Hasan (q), Abu Ali (q), Yusuf (q), Abul Abbas al-Khidr (as), and Abdul Khaliq (q).

12

Arif ar-Rivgari (q)

Shaykh Arif (q) was born in the village of Rivgar, which lies six miles outside the city of Bukhara and only one mile from Ghujdawan. He stood at the door of his shaykh, Abdul Khaliq (q), and served him faithfully from childhood. The Shaykh gave him permission to guide others. He became a deputy to Abdul Khaliq (q) until the latter's death. At that time the secret of the Golden Chain was passed to him.

Shaykh Arif (q) lived and died in the small village into which he was born. He taught there the eight principles of his teacher and he was perfect in his example of following those principles. He avoided the society of men and shunned any recognition or fame. He made God his only goal and the awareness of death his only companion.

He said that there are three kinds of hearts that characterize the believers. The first heart is like a mountain, which nothing can move. The second heart is like a palm tree whose roots are firmly planted in the ground but whose branches sway in the wind. The third type of heart is like a feather, which is blown here and there at the whim of any breeze.

For over sixty years he taught whoever came to him the method of strengthening and steadying the heart. He was a lover of God and a true servant of his Shaykh. He left this world to join them in 636 AH / 1238 CE. He passed the secret of the Golden Chain to his student Mahmud al-Injir al-Faghnawi (q).

May Allah bless an-Nabi (sas), as-Siddiq (ra), Salman (ra), Qasim (ra), Jafar (ra), Tayfur (q), Abul Hasan (q), Abu Ali (q), Yusuf (q), Abul Abbas al-Khidr (as), Abdul Khaliq (q), and Arif (q).

74 Links of Light: The Golden Chain

Mahmoud al-Injir al-Faghnawi

13

Mahmoud al-Injir al-Faghnawi (q)

Like Shaykh Arif (q), Mahmoud (q) lived and died just miles from the town into which he was born. This town, called Injir Faghna, was just three miles from Bukhara. In the evenings it was his practice to attend the gatherings of his Shaykh and sit at his feet. During the day he worked as a carpenter in the city of Bukhara.

It was said that Shaykh Mahmoud (q) held the stations of two prophets. He occupied the station of knowledge of God belonging to the Prophet Muhammad (sas) and he also occupied the station of talking directly with God that belonged to the Prophet Musa (as).

Because of the condition of the people in his time, he reinstituted the practice of public, or voiced dhikr, in addition to keeping the secret dhikr of Shaykh Abdul Khaliq (q). When questioned about why he returned to loud dhikr he replied, "In order to waken the sleeper." Since secret dhikr must remain secret it is not possible to perform it publicly.

Shaykh Mahmoud (q) was also an intimate of Khidr (as) and they spent much time in each other's company. Sayyidina Khidr (as) brought a young man named, Ali ar-Ramitani (q), to meet the Shaykh and be trained by him. One afternoon many years later, when Shaykh Ali (q) was sitting within a circle of students, a white bird came and sat directly on his head. It opened its beak and spoke in clear human language for all to hear. It said, "O Ali, be brave, do not abandon manliness!" The students were so shocked to hear words come from the beak of a bird that they all fainted. When they came to their senses, they questioned Shaykh

Ali (q). He explained that the white bird was actually Shaykh Mahmoud (q) to whom Allah had given many extraordinary powers, including the ability to fly.

Whoever sat in the company of Shaykh Mahmoud (q) felt all his troubles melt away. Joy would fill his heart and sweet laughter would fill his throat. When Shaykh Nazim (q) (Chapter 40) visited the tomb of Shaykh Mahmoud (q) in Uzbekistan in 2003 his companions saw him suddenly begin to smile, then his shoulders begin to shake with silent laughter. It was only later that the old caretaker of the mosque explained to them that Shaykh Nazim (q) must have been in the spiritual company of Shaykh Mahmoud (q), because it was known in the village that when he was alive all people reacted in this joyful way to his company.

Shaykh Mahmoud (q) died in the vicinity of Bukhara on the seventeenth of *Rabi al-Awwal* in the year 717 AH / 1317 CE. He poured the secret of the Golden Chain into the heart of his student, Ali ar-Ramitani (q).

May Allah bless an-Nabi (sas), as-Siddiq (ra), Salman (ra), Qasim (ra), Jafar (ra), Tayfur (q), Abul Hasan (q), Abu Ali (q), Yusuf (q), Abul Abbas al-Khidr (as), Abdul Khaliq (q), Arif (q), and Mahmoud (q).

14
Ali ar-Ramitani, Azizan (q)

Shaykh Ali (q) was born in Ramitan on the outskirts of Bukhara. He studied the Quran, Hadith and Islamic law at the university there. Bukhara had become a center of both international trade and Muslim scholarship. Shaykh Ali (q) achieved success in his studies and was on his way to becoming a teacher and lawmaker when he sought out the spiritual path at the door of Mahmud al-Injir al-Faghnawi (q). He became his devoted disciple and into his heart was poured the secrets of the Golden Chain. He was called "Azizan," a title meaning, "the loved one," and acknowledging his lofty spiritual state.

Although highly educated, Azizan (q) continued to practice a trade for a living. He was a weaver of cloth. At one point he was ordered by Allah to move to the city of Khwarazm. He traveled to the city and set up camp outside the gates. He sent a disciple to the Shah, the king of Khwarazm. The disciple was instructed to announce that a weaver was asking his royal permission to live in his city. The disciple was also instructed to insist on the Shah's response in writing. The Shah was amused by this elaborate request from a simple weaver. He granted the request with a letter, signed and sealed. Only upon receiving it did Azizan (q) move through the gates and into Khwarazm.

He rented a small house in the corner of the city and began to work. Everyday he would go to the central square where men, who were looking to be hired as day laborers, sat and waited. Azizan (q) hired several and brought them back to his house. There he asked them to wash and make *wudu* and together they prayed and recited dhikr. Afterwards he fed them and paid them their wages. Of course the men of the city recognized a good deal when they saw one. Everyday, men competed with each other for the chance to go home with Ali Azizan (q). They fell in love with his gentle manner and the light shining from his face. Once they had been in his company they could no longer stay away.

Soon the whole city of Khwarazm sat at the feet of Ali Azizan (q) and he taught them dhikr and the Naqshbandi way. The advisors of the Shah began to get concerned that the Shaykh had too much power. They voiced their concerns to the Shah. The Shah sent for the Shaykh. Azizan (q) had anticipated such an event and he carried the Shah's written permission at all times in his pocket. Now he took it out and showed it to the court. The light shining from Azizan (q) captivated the Shah and he also accepted Ali Azizan (q) as his shaykh. The whole city now glowed with peace and blessings.

Azizan (q), like his Shaykh before him, led his students in public dhikr. When questioned about this he replied that reciting dhikr out loud is helpful for the beginner because it serves to drown out the noise of the world on the outside and the thoughts of the world on the inside. A beginner's heart is easily distracted and unstable. After years of doing dhikr, however, the heart is strengthened and steadied. At that point the dhikr done on the heart in secret becomes essential.

One day an important man came to visit the Shaykh. Ali Azizan (q) had not a morsel of food in his kitchen with which to serve his guest. He was very sad. Just then a young man arrived with a pot of stew he was bringing as a gift. Azizan (q) was delighted. After the guest had eaten and gone, the Shaykh offered to pray to Allah to grant whatever the boy might wish for. The boy thought long and hard and then replied that his only desire was to become just like Ali Azizan (q) himself.

Ali Azizan (q) warned the boy that high spiritual states are accompanied by heavy responsibilities and burdens. The boy persisted in his desire, saying that there was nothing else in the entire world that he wanted. So Azizan (q) prayed to Allah and, little by little over the next month, the boy changed. Inwardly and outwardly the boy began to resemble the Shaykh in every way. After forty days in this state the boy died. He was unable to support the spiritual burdens of the Shaykh, but he died in happiness, having attained everlasting joy.

Ali Azizan (q) lived one hundred and thirty (130) years. He died and was buried in Khwarazm in the year 721 AH / 1321 CE. He left two sons of high spiritual station, but he passed the Secret of the Golden Chain to Muhammad Baba as-Samasi (q).

May Allah bless an-Nabi (sas), as-Siddiq (ra), Salman (ra), Qasim (ra), Jafar (ra), Tayfur (q), Abul Hasan (q), Abu Ali (q), Yusuf (q), Abul Abbas al-Khidr (as), Abdul Khaliq (q), Arif (q), Mahmoud (q), and Ali (q).

82 Links of Light: The Golden Chain

15

Muhammad Baba as-Samasi (q)

Muhammad Baba as-Samasi (q) was born in the village of Samas, near Ramitan and just a few miles outside the city of Bukhara, in what is now Uzbekistan. He studied the Quran and Hadith, becoming an accomplished scholar of Islamic Law. Then he went on to study history, logic and philosophy until he was a walking encyclopedia of every kind of art and science.

He sat at the feet of Shaykh Ali ar-Ramitani, Azizan (q), fasting by day and praying by night. He kept himself in seclusion except for the company of his Shaykh. When his heart opened, Ali Azizan (q) poured into it the secrets of the Golden Chain. Shaykh Muhammad (q) used to stress the importance of finding a living shaykh because he knew that the guidance of a real shaykh is a much more effective method of learning than reading books.

Shaykh Muhammad (q) related that once he went to visit Ali Azizan (q) and was plunged into a state of spiritual vision. Shaykh Muhammad (q) no longer saw before his eyes the reception room of Azizan (q) but instead he saw an open road. He began to walk. He traveled down this road for many days until he saw before him the beautiful octagonal mosque known as the Dome of the Rock. Sayyidina Omar (ra) built this mosque over the rock on which the Beloved Prophet (sas) dismounted from the *Buraq* (as) on the Night Journey (called in Arabic, *Isra*). From this rock the Prophet (sas) rose into the heavens accompanied by the Archangel Jibrail (as), a journey that is called the *Mihraj*.

Shaykh Muhammad (q) was welcomed at the door of the mosque by a man who was dressed all in green. The Green Man (as) told him that he and Ali Azizan (q) had been waiting a long time for him to arrive. It was the anniversary of the Prophet's (sas) *Mihraj*, the 27th of *Rajab*, exactly three months to the day since he had entered the Shaykh's house in Ramitan. After praying the night prayer, Azizan (q) led Shaykh Muhammad (q) outside where the Man in Green (as) presented them with two *buraq* steeds. They mounted and rose up into the heavens. There they retraced the Prophet's (sas) journey until they arrived at the Lotus Tree of the Farthest Boundary.

They saw things too strange and wonderful to put into words but Shaykh Muhammad (q) did say later that when they arrived at the Divine Presence everything vanished. He understood that in that place nothing truly exists except the Prophet (sas) and beyond him, only Allah Almighty Himself. The Prophet (sas) talked to him and told him to return to his normal life and serve as a guide for those struggling without vision. At this point Shaykh Muhammad (q) closed his eyes. When he opened them again he was back in Azizan's (q) house in Uzbekistan. No time had elapsed although he had experienced every detail of a journey of many months.

Even though he was trained as a scholar and teacher, he worked every day in his gardens. He had a small orchard behind his house and it was his practice to prune the trees himself. It is said that every time he cut a branch Allah opened for him another secret. This spiritual experience would sometimes so overwhelm him that the pruning knife would fall abruptly from his hands.

One day while traveling with his disciples through the neighboring villages, he stopped before a small house. It was in a place called "Fort of the Indians" (Qasr al-Hindi). He marveled at the sweet spiritual scent he could smell there. He told his companions that soon a great hero would be born in this place. The village would change its name because of him and forever after be known as "Fort of the Knower" (Qasr al-Arifan). The spiritual path they followed would also be known by his name. In fact he would leave his mark on the whole world.

Some years later Shaykh Muhammad (q) passed by this village again. The scent was so strong that he knew immediately that the baby he had been waiting for had been born. He knocked at the door. An old man brought his three-day-old grandson to receive the blessings of the Shaykh. Shaykh Muhammad (q) fixed his gaze upon the radiant child and declared, "This is my son. I have known of him for a long, long time." Then, turning to his companions, he explained that Allah had put His stamp or mark (naqsh) on this child's heart and this child would leave its impression on the rest of the world.

Shaykh Muhammad (q) turned to one of his companions named Amir Kulal (q) and ordered him to watch over and guide this child who he said would in turn be a guide for all humanity and a leader of the people who love God. Amir Kulal (q) humbly accepted this task and promised to train and protect the child, who would come to be known as Bahauddin an-Naqshband (q).

Muhammad Baba as-Samasi (q) died in 755 AH / 1354 CE in his birthplace of Samas. He passed the secret of the Golden Chain to his companion Sayyid Amir Kulal (q).

May Allah bless an-Nabi (sas), as-Siddiq (ra), Salman (ra), Qasim (ra), Jafar (ra), Tayfur (q), Abul Hasan (q), Abu Ali (q), Yusuf (q), Abul Abbas al-Khidr (as), Abdul Khaliq (q), Arif (q), Mahmoud (q), Ali (q), and Muhammad Baba as-Samasi (q).

86 Links of Light: The Golden Chain

16

Sayyid Amir Kulal (q)

Sayyid Amir Kulal (q) was born in the village of Sukhar, two miles from Bukhara. He was a descendant of the noble Prophet Muhammad (sas) and this is why he is called by the honorary title, "Sayyid." When his mother was pregnant with him she noticed that whenever she tried to eat food from a doubtful source, grown or cooked by people who were not believers, or food bought with money that was not earned in a lawful way, her stomach became upset and she could not eat. As long as she chose carefully from the best and definitely lawful foods she had no problems. She realized right away that she carried inside of her a very special soul.

In his youth, Sayyid Amir (q) loved to wrestle. He was strong and an excellent athlete. At that time wrestling was one of the most popular sports. There were open stadiums where crowds would gather to watch and even gamble on their favorite fighters. Sayyid Amir (q) became the local champion. The other wrestlers would study his fights into order to learn better techniques.

One day a man watching the wrestling match began to have questions in his heart. How could it be that a descendant of the Prophet (sas) and an accomplished scholar such as Sayyid Amir (q) could show himself in public in such an undignified way and allow himself to become the center of such unlawful activity? Just then this man began to experience a terrible fear as if the Last Days had arrived and he was facing the Judgment of his Lord. He felt like he was in a sea of mud struggling to keep from sinking, unable to pull himself free. Just as the mud was about to suck him under he saw the strong arms of Sayyid Amir (q) reaching out to pull him to safety. "Yes," said Sayyid Amir (q) in answer to the man's unspoken question, "We practice wrestling in order to be strong enough to rescue someone like you!"

Many months later Shaykh Muhammad Baba as-Samasi (q) was passing by the wrestling stadium. To the astonishment of his companions he stopped and began watching the activity from a far corner. He fixed his eyes on Sayyid Amir (q) so intensely that after a few moments Sayyid Amir (q) became aware of the Shaykh. He turned to face him and their eyes connected. Sayyid Amir (q) froze in the middle of his match. The gaze of the Shaykh penetrated deep into his heart, awakening a love and a longing that he had never experienced before. Shaykh Muhammad (q) abruptly turned away and left the stadium, followed by his puzzled companions. Sayyid Amir (q) remained, frozen and stunned. After a few minutes he fled the wrestling stadium and followed Shaykh Muhammad (q). When he caught up with him he clung to the hem of his robe, gasping for breath.

After this Sayyid Amir (q) remained in the service of Shaykh Muhammad (q), learning from him the practice of dhikr and the principles of the Way. For twenty years he stayed in virtual seclusion. He abandoned worldly pleasures. He never went near the wrestling stadium, the bazaar or even the market. He stayed either in his own house or he walked the five miles to visit his Shaykh. When his heart opened Shaykh Muhammad (q) poured into it the secrets of the Golden Chain.

It was into the strong hands of Sayyid Amir (q) that Shaykh Muhammad (q) entrusted the care of the great soul of Bahauddin an-Naqshband (q). When Bahauddin (q) was still a baby Shaykh Muhammad (q) took a promise from Sayyid Amir (q) to watch over and train him with the greatest of care. Sayyid Amir (q) raised Bahauddin (q) as his spiritual son. He fulfilled his promise to his Shaykh and when he died in the village of Sukhar on the eight of *Jumada al-Awwal* in the year 772 AH / 1370 CE he poured the secrets of the Golden Chain into the heart of Bahauddin an-Naqshband (q).

May Allah bless an-Nabi (sas), as-Siddiq (ra), Salman (ra), Qasim (ra), Jafar (ra), Tayfur (q), Abul Hasan (q), Abu Ali (q), Yusuf (q), Abul Abbas al-Khidr (as), Abdul Khaliq (q), Arif (q), Mahmoud (q), Ali (q), Muhammad Baba as-Samasi (q), and Sayyid Amir Kulal (q).

Sayyid Amir Kulal (q)

90 Links of Light: The Golden Chain

17
Muhammad Bahauddin Shah Naqshband (q)

Shah Naqshband (q) was born in Qasr al-Arifan near Bukhara on the seventeenth of *Muharram* 717 AH / 1317 CE. He was given the name Bahauddin that means, Beauty of the Religion, and he would come to decorate the earth and its people with the pearls and gems of heavenly knowledge. He was called Naqshband because he became the means by which Allah would mark (*naqsh*) the hearts of all living things. He was called Shah because he was the king of the saints and shaykhs of the Golden Chain. In his honor they still call themselves by his name, Naqshbandi.

His first teacher was Muhammad Baba as-Samasi (q) who held and blessed him soon after he was born. His second teacher was Sayyid Amir Kulal (q) who raised him as a son. But his primary guides into the highest of spiritual realms were those who had gone on before. Uways al-Qarni (as) gave him support and guidance. Abdul Khaliq al-Ghujdawani (q), who had died two hundred years earlier, was his companion and teacher. For this reason Shah Naqshband (q) was called *Uwaysi*.

When he was four he amazed his family and neighbors by being able to see things that were hidden to others. He could see the babies in the wombs of their mothers, both human and animal, and so tell people what to expect.

In the world of the spirit there are no ages. The spirit is not born nor does it grow old. It is ageless and timeless. When he was just seven he was taken spiritually to meet the souls of the Messengers of God, including the Prophet Muhammad (sas). He was introduced to all the Prophets and he respectfully answered their questions. He was then introduced to all the Saints of the Golden Chain. At this time he had the opportunity to ask Allah to promise to give special guidance to all those who would follow him, both in the present and in the future. All the angels seconded his request with their "Amin."

In his youth he would rise early, at least three hours before the morning prayer. During the day he would fast and either stay in the company of his Shaykh or worship in seclusion. He paid no attention to material things, not to the state of his clothes or even to the state of his body. He wandered the graveyards during the freezing Uzbeki nights, without warm clothes or shoes, learning from the dead. His guides spoke directly to his heart and he followed them without paying any attention to the conditions of the world around him or to the opinions of others. His only goal was the pleasure of Allah Almighty.

One day he was in a state of Divine Attraction and unaware of anything except what was happening in his heart. He moved from here to there, not conscious of what he was doing or where he was going until night fell. His feet had become torn and bloody from the thorns and the rocks on the ground. In the darkness he made his way to the house of his Shaykh, Sayyid Amir Kulal (q). When the Shaykh saw his filthy and ragged condition he ordered his companions to throw him out. "I do not want him in my house," he said.

Bahauddin (q) felt his heart break and his pride and anger rise. He knew his hurt feelings were like a poison that would kill his trust in and love for his Shaykh and he fought those feelings. He begged Allah to help him carry this hurt and humiliation. Later he said, "I put humbleness at the door of pride and placed my head on the step of the door of Sayyid Amir Kulal (q) and vowed to stay there until he would accept me again."

The snow began to fall. The night was pitch black without moon or stars to give comfort or light. The single outer garment he wore was a tattered leather cloak. Only his love for his Shaykh warmed him from the inside against the frigid air.

At dawn the Shaykh opened the door and put his foot on Bahauddin's (q) head, which had become covered with snow and almost indistinguishable from the step. The Shaykh sensed the presence of Bahauddin (q) and withdrew his foot. He lifted his frozen student from the ground and brought him inside. With great care Shaykh Amir Kulal (q) removed the thorns from Bahauddin's (q) feet and bandaged them. He wrapped him in blankets and set him by the fire. As he did this he poured into Bahauddin's (q) heart his store of Heavenly secrets.

Bahauddin (q) saw himself enter the secret of *Muhammad Rasulullah*. This led him to the secret of *La ilaha illa Allah*. This led him to the secret of God's Names and Attributes that are expressed by the secret of God's Oneness. Such secrets cannot be known by words but only by the taste experienced in the heart of the knower.

After many years of study and effort, Shah Naqshband (q) settled in Bukhara and built a mosque and school. People came from all over to study with him or just to receive his blessing. When he had been quite young he had been taught by Abdul Khaliq al-Ghujdawani (q) the practice of the silent dhikr. After this he was unable to sit, even in the company of his Shaykh, and do dhikr out loud in public. In the way of Abdul Khaliq (q) he taught the secret dhikr and the eight principles, to which he added three more principles.

The three additional principles of the Naqshbandi Way that come from Shah Naqshband (q) are:

9. <u>Awareness</u> of <u>Time</u>. Keep watch over every precious second Allah has given you and spend it carefully in His way. For every moment there is a proper attitude. When you are sad you must ask for forgiveness for the things you have done to earn such sadness. When you are happy you must give thanks to Allah for all He has given you. Time is marked by the continual movement between these two states, expansion and contraction, like breathing in and breathing out. Be aware of the passing of time and the condition of your self within it.

10. <u>Awareness</u> of <u>Number</u>. Count the times you recite God's Holy Name. Especially in the silent dhikr keep count of the repetitions. On a basic level this practice keeps

you from being distracted by the world. On a higher level, awareness of number becomes awareness of the Number: One. Allah is One. In the absence of One no other numbers exist. All creation is in need of the only One.

11. <u>Awareness of the Heart</u>. The dhikr is concentrated inside the heart, which is the center of power. All thoughts and emotions pass through the heart like a stormy ocean overwhelming the shore. Dhikr is what brings calm to the heart, making the waves of thoughts and emotions, both good and bad, run smoothly and rhythmically. This keeps the shore of the heart firm and secure allowing for the undisturbed awareness that in reality there is only Allah.

It is said that Shah Naqshband (q), when he got older, was short and quite round. He had an extremely long, white beard. If you were lucky enough to look into his eyes, they appeared to spin around like wheels of light.

As he had shown his students the perfect way to live, now he showed them also the perfect way to die. After instructing them to dig his grave in the garden of his mosque, Shah Naqshband (q) recited *Sura Ya Sin*, passed his blessed hand over his radiant face and returned to his Lord. It was the third of *Rabi' al-Awwal*, 791 AH / 1388 CE. He poured the secrets of the Golden Chain into the heart of Alauddin al-Attar (q).

May Allah bless an-Nabi (sas), as-Siddiq (ra), Salman (ra), Qasim (ra), Jafar (ra), Tayfur (q), Abul Hasan (q), Abu Ali (q), Yusuf (q), Abul Abbas al-Khidr (as), Abdul Khaliq (q), Arif (q), Mahmoud (q), Ali (q) Muhammad Baba as-Samasi (q), Sayyid Amir Kulal (q), and Shah Bahauddin an-Naqshband (q).

18
Alauddin al-Attar (q)

Alauddin (q) was born to a prominent family in the city of Bukhara. At an early age he dedicated himself to seeking the knowledge that would bring him closer to Allah. He studied at the Islamic university under many of the most famous scholars of his time. When his father died, Shaykh Alauddin (q) gave all of his sizeable inheritance to his two brothers and continued to live as a humble student. When his accomplishments started to be recognized by those around him he retreated from their company. He began to spend more and more time outside the city sitting and learning at the feet of Shah Naqshband (q).

One night Shah Naqshband (q) saw a vision in which the Prophet (sas) ordered him to marry his youngest daughter to Shaykh Alauddin (q). It was the middle of the night but the venerable Shah Naqshband (q) put on his cloak, took his staff and made his way through the frozen streets to the vicinity of the university. There he found all in darkness except for a faint light glimmering in a corner room. Shah Naqshband (q) entered the room and found inside only a straw mat spread on the hard floor for a bed, two bricks for a pillow, and a cracked jar in which to store water. The young Alauddin (q) was reading the Quran by the dim light of a tiny oil lamp. Shah Naqshband (q) greeted him but got no response. He greeted him again but still the reading figure did not respond.

Then Shah Naqshband (q) greeted Alauddin (q) in a spiritual way. Shaykh Alauddin (q) finally heard and answered immediately. He rose and kissed the hands and feet of his shaykh. When Shaykh Alauddin (q) heard the good news that the Prophet (sas) had chosen him to marry Shah Naqshband's (q) daughter he was very happy. He was also worried because he had nothing with which to support a wife and family. Shah Naqshband (q) assured him that whatever they needed Allah would provide.

As his teacher, Shah Naqshband (q) had to make sure that no pride entered the heart of Shaykh Alauddin (q), especially now that he had been chosen to be his son-in-law. Pride belongs only to the master not to the servant. Pride is the one thing that can close our hearts and prevent us from becoming what we were created to be, servants of Allah Almighty.

Shah Naqshband (q) ordered Shaykh Alauddin (q) to fill a large tray with apples and balance it on his head. Then he ordered him to walk about the public market of Bukhara barefoot, calling out at the top of his lungs, "Apples for sale. Apples for sale." Although this was a humiliating activity for any man of good family and education, Alauddin (q) obeyed his teacher with an easy and joyful heart. His brothers, however, were horrified. They felt humiliated for him and by him. They felt ashamed that a member of their family should be seen by the whole world as a barefoot street vendor. They complained to the Shaykh. Shah Naqshband (q) immediately ordered Alauddin (q) to stop walking about the marketplace selling his apples. He ordered him instead to sit down and sell his apples on the doorstep of his brothers' fancy store.

Shah Naqshband (q) tested Shaykh Alauddin (q) in many ways. He kept him close to his side in order to monitor the state of his heart at all times. Eventually he trusted him enough to turn over the training of many of his followers and he used to publicly express thanks for his help. After Shah Naqshband (q) died, Shaykh Alauddin (q) was recognized by all to be the next link in the Golden Chain, the inheritor of the light and the secret.

Sometime later there arose a heated argument among the scholars of Bukhara. Some said that Allah could be seen in this world and some that He could not be seen. They came to Shaykh Alauddin (q) to settle their disagreement. They knew that he had both the scholarly learning and the inner wisdom to decide between them. He told all the scholars who did not believe that Allah could be seen, to wash and join him in his mosque. If they kept completely silent he promised them a decision within three days. On the third day such a state of wonder overcame them that those stately scholars began to roll on the floor in fits of joy. When they came to themselves they knew absolutely that the vision of Allah in this world is possible because they had seen it. They kissed the hands and feet of Shaykh Alauddin (q) who had enabled them to witness this truth, and they went on to serve him for the rest of their lives.

Shaykh Alauddin (q) continued to teach from his mosque in Bukhara and many books were written about his scholarly advice and spiritual wisdom. On the second day of the month of *Rajab* 1400 CE, Shaykh Alauddin (q) announced, "I am going to leave you to go to another life and no one can stop me." He died on the twentieth day of that very month and was buried near where he taught. He passed the light and the secret to his longtime companion and disciple, Shaykh Ya'qub al-Charkhi (q).

Forty days after his death a student saw him in a dream. (If you see one of the shaykhs in a dream it must be real because Allah would not allow anything false or imaginary to take the shape of one of His saints.) Shaykh Alauddin (q) put a long sharp needle upright in the ground, placed his foot on its tip and stood up. He said sainthood belongs to the one who can stand steadily on the point of a needle without swaying either to one side or the other.

God bless an-Nabi (sas), as-Siddiq (ra), Salman (ra), Qasim (ra), Jafar (ra), Tayfur (q), Abul Hasan (q), Abu Ali (q), Yusuf (q), Abul Abbas al-Khidr (as), Abdul Khaliq (q), Arif (q), Mahmoud (q), Ali (q), Muhammad Baba as-Samasi (q), Sayyid Amir Kulal (q), Shah Bahauddin an-Naqshband (q), and Alauddin (q).

19
Ya'qub al-Charkhi (q)

Shaykh Ya'qub (q) was born in the village of Charkh, which lies between Kandahar and Kabul in what is now Afghanistan. He went to Herat to study the Islamic sciences and from there he went to Egypt. He memorized all of the Quran, half a million hadith and all the history that goes with them. He studied until he was one of the few men at that time qualified to make legal decisions on any matter that concerned the Muslim community.

Shaykh Ya'qub (q) decided to return home to serve his own people. On his way back to Charkh, he stopped in Bukhara to visit Shah Naqshband (q). Because of his great reputation and the fact that all people, whatever their differences, agreed in their respect for him, Ya'qub (q) asked to be accepted as a student of Shah Naqshband (q).

But Shah Naqshband (q) did not find that a sufficient reason to accept Ya'qub (q) as his student. In those days the Shaykh did not automatically give *bayat*, initiation, to anyone who asked. Many, many seekers were refused. Shaykh Ya'qub (q) quoted a hadith that says, "If God loves someone He will influence the hearts of people to love that person as well." Shah Naqshband (q) smiled and said that he was in fact the inheritor of "the loved one" (Azizan in Arabic). Shaykh Ya'qub (q) was startled. He had, until that moment, forgotten a dream he had had several weeks earlier in which a voice had ordered him to "follow Azizan (q)". Shah Naqshband (q) had reminded him of his own dream.

Shah Naqshband (q) did not yet accept him but he told him that if he happened to meet a certain saint on his way back to Charkh he should be careful to keep his mind and heart free of gossip in his presence. Shaykh Ya'qub (q) had no intention to visit this saint. The village in which the saint lived was not even near the road he was intending to travel.

But his caravan, without his knowledge, made a detour and he found himself in the village of the saint nevertheless. It was dark when they arrived. Shaykh Ya'qub (q) went to the mosque, hoping to find someone to give him directions to the saint's house. As he entered, a man came out from behind a pillar and asked if he was Ya'qub (q). The man had been inspired by Shah Naqshband (q) to wait at the mosque in order to take Ya'qub (q) directly to the saint.

Finally at the saint's house, Shaykh Ya'qub (q) struggled with great difficulty to keep his mind and heart clear of gossip. The saint gave to Shaykh Ya'qub (q) a piece of spiritual knowledge that he had never heard before. Ya'qub (q) was very happy and thanked his shaykh, Shah Naqshband (q), who he realized had arranged the whole event, even changing the route of the caravan, just for his benefit.

Shaykh Ya'qub (q) continued on to Charkh where he became established as an Imam and scholar. From time to time he would go to Bukhara to visit Shah Naqshband (q). One day on his way to visit his shaykh he stopped to ask for the blessing of a dervish, a saint so absorbed in his love for Allah that he cared for nothing else, not weather, not wealth, not the opinions of people. This dervish lived like a crazy person in the streets. Only those able to really see knew that he was not mad, but rather madly in love with God. The man began to draw lines in the dust of the road. It came to Shaykh Ya'qub's (q) heart to count these lines. If they added up to an odd number he felt his intention would be blessed. Allah is One and He loves the odd number. Shaykh Ya'qub counted the lines and to his immense happiness he found them to be odd.

When he reached the mosque Shah Naqshband (q) was waiting for him. He commented on Ya'qub's (q) happiness about the odd number, indicating that he already knew about the dervish and the lines in the dust. Then he took Shaykh Ya'qub (q) into the secrets of the station of the tenth Principle, Awareness of Number. He instructed Shaykh Ya'qub (q) to try always to be aware of the odd number.

Later that night, Shah Naqshband (q) was finally ordered by Allah to accept Shaykh Ya'qub (q) into his way. Shaykh Ya'qub (q) said that when Shah Naqshband (q) looked at him to tell him the good news he felt himself disappear. Wherever he looked, inside or outside, he saw only Shah Naqshband (q). Then Shah Naqshband (q) began to recite the names of the Shaykhs of the Golden Chain: The Prophet (sas), Siddiq, Salman, Qasim, Jafar, Tayfur, Abul Hassan, Abu Ali, Yusuf, Abul Abbas, Abdul Khaliq (qhum). As he mentioned their names each shaykh appeared before Shaykh Ya'qub (q). When Abdul Khaliq (q) appeared he paused to teach Shaykh Ya'qub (q) something more about the Awareness of Number. Then Shah Naqshband (q) continued: Arif, Mahmoud, Ali, Muhammad Baba as-Samasi, Sayyid Amir Kulal (qhum). Each one appeared and gave his hand and his blessing to Shaykh Ya'qub (q). This is the reality of initiation although most of us are not able to experience it as he did.

Shaykh Ya'qub (q) stayed in Bukhara after that, by the side of Shah Naqshband (q) until his death. Then, following his orders, he took the hand of Shaykh Alauddin al-Attar (q) and served him until he reached spiritual perfection.

Shaykh Ya'qub (q) was known to lose consciousness of the world when certain spiritual truths were revealed to him. Even his fellow students had noticed this while they were studying together in Egypt. He had the habit of combing his long beard with his fingers. Sometimes the state of unconsciousness would come upon him so suddenly that his hand would fall like a rock into his lap, pulling with it a tassel of long beard hairs. Yet he would feel nothing because he was so absorbed in his spiritual vision.

Shaykh Ya'qub (q) died on the fifth of the month of *Safar* in 851 AH / 1447 CE and was buried in the village of Khulgatu. He passed the secret of the Golden Chain to his companion, UbaydAllah al-Ahrar (q).

May Allah bless an-Nabi (sas), as-Siddiq (ra), Salman (ra), Qasim (ra), Jafar (ra), Tayfur (q), Abul Hasan (q), Abu Ali (q), Yusuf (q), Abul Abbas al-Khidr (as), Abdul Khaliq (q), Arif (q), Mahmoud (q), Ali (q), Muhammad Baba as-Samasi (q), Sayyid Amir Kulal (q), Shah Bahauddin an-Naqshband (q), Alauddin (q), and Ya'qub (q).

Ya'qub al-Charkhi (q) 105

106 Links of Light: The Golden Chain

20
Ubaydallah al-Ahrar (q)

In the village of Shash, in the vicinity of Samarkand, there lived a young husband and wife. One day the man began to change. He became very religious. He began to fast all day and pray all night until his family feared that he had given up food and sleep altogether. He devoted himself entirely to his shaykh and his spiritual practices. After some months in this condition he was inspired to go to his wife. She became pregnant. As soon as the child was conceived the unusual spiritual condition left the father. He became like he was before, a good man of average spiritual ambition.

Nine months later, in the month of Ramadan, 806 AH /1404 CE, a baby boy was born to this young couple. They named him, UbaydAllah (q). He refused to nurse from his mother until her forty days had finished and she was able to resume her prayers. The baby had such a radiant face that anyone who saw him was drawn to him and prayed from their heart for his good fortune. Even as a tiny infant the name of Allah was always on his tongue. As he grew into a young boy his heart remained always in remembrance of his Lord and he thought that this was the natural state of everyone around him.

One stormy day while walking to school his foot sank deep into the mud of the road. While struggling to get his shoe free he managed to also get the hem of his long quilted winter coat caught in the mud. Twisting and turning, slipping and sliding, for the first time in his life, he forgot Allah in the effort to free himself from the mud. When he realized what had happened he burst into tears.

He assumed that all other people around him were constant in their remembrance and that he was the only one who was heedless and forgetful. It was not until much later that he became aware that the reality was actually quite different. Most people spend their lives in forgetfulness with a few true moments of remembering Allah. UbaydAllah (q) spent most of his life in remembrance with only these few moments of heedlessness.

The other boys would try to get him to play games with them between classes at school. But he would stand, alone by himself, wrapped in his own state of closeness to God. As he grew older he began spending more time in the graveyards in the company of the saintly dead. They were the only ones who shared his complete absorption in the worship of Allah. They taught him from their stores of wisdom.

He followed their advice and treated everyone he met as if he might be Khidr (as) and every night he worshipped as if that night might be *Lailatul Qadr* (the Night of Power, on which the Quran was revealed and on which any righteous wish may be granted). He humbled himself before everyone, kissed the hem of their robe and begged them to ask Allah to forgive him. He assumed that their prayers were more likely to be granted than his. Every night he spent absorbed in prayer and dhikr.

During the day he farmed his mother's land. He sold the produce in the local markets. During all his interactions with people he heard only the sound of dhikr. The chatter and gossip of the crowds in the marketplace sounded to him like dhikr. The music and rowdy celebration of a wedding feast came to his ears as dhikr. The whistling of the wind, the chirping of the birds, the creaking of the wagon wheel, all sounded to him like dhikr. He never in his life heard anything other than dhikr.

Although in his youth he was very poor, he refused to accept any charity from anyone. He even refused invitations to eat in the houses of kindly people. Never in his whole life did he even accept a gift. His name UbaydAllah means Servant of Allah. It was his goal in life to become the perfect exemplar of that name. His path was service to those more in need than he. He nursed the sick, sheltered the poor and fed the hungry. When he became a famous shaykh with many followers, including the Sultan, he continued to sacrifice himself for the comfort of others. Because of his generosity, Allah increased Shaykh UbaydAllah (q) in wealth and property until his accountants could no longer keep count, and the amount he paid in taxes served to support the entire state. Whatever entered his storehouses increased in value and everything he had he put at the service of others.

During his lifetime the political situation in his region was very unstable and dangerous. The mighty king and conquorer, Tamerlane, had just died. His descendants fought with each other to be king with no regard for what war and disruption of trade would do to the kingdom. Shaykh UbaydAllah (q) spent his time and his energy in the service of the people in this aspect also. He put his enormous spiritual power behind the prince who promised to treat the people with mercy and uphold God's Law. He made peace where possible and where it was not possible, he led the most just of the warring princes to victory.

Shaykh UbaydAllah (q) accompanied the Prince to the battlefield, giving him explicit instructions for defeating the enemy. He sent his deputies onto the towers of their besieged city to concentrate on dhikr until devastating winds and disease scattered the attacking army. The Prince put his complete trust in the guidance of the Shaykh. Many say that a holy man should avoid the company of the rich and powerful. Shaykh UbaydAllah (q) said that it would be a sin for him not to give his attention to them since Allah had given him the power to guide even the rulers to the right path.

At the age of eighty-nine (89) Shaykh UbaydAllah (q) became ill. On a Friday in the month of *Rabi' al-Awwal* in the year 859 AH / 1490 CE, after praying the night prayer, people saw a light flash beneath the eyelids of Shaykh UbaydAllah (q). This light was so bright that the lamp-lit room appeared dark in comparison. Then he left this world as he had entered it, with the name of Allah on his breath. He was buried beside his mosque and school, near the soup kitchen he had founded to feed the poor. The Sultan helped carry his body to its final resting place, followed by all of the army and all of the people. He passed the secret of the Golden Chain to Shaykh Muhammad az-Zahid al-Qadi as-Samarqandi (q).

May Allah bless an-Nabi (sas), as-Siddiq (ra), Salman (ra), Qasim (ra), Jafar (ra), Tayfur (q), Abul Hasan (q), Abu Ali (q), Yusuf (q), Abul Abbas al-Khidr (as), Abdul Khaliq (q), Arif (q), Mahmoud (q), Ali (q), Muhammad Baba as-Samasi (q), Sayyid Amir Kulal (q), Shah Bahauddin an-Naqshband (q), Alauddin (q), Ya'qub (q), and UbaydAllah (q).

110　Links of Light: The Golden Chain

Ubaydallah al-Ahrar (q) 111

112 Links of Light: The Golden Chain

21

Muhammad az-Zahid (q)

Muhammad (q) was a devoted disciple of Shaykh UbaydAllah (q). In 883 AH / 1478 CE Muhammad (q) was traveling with a friend, from his home in Samarkand to Herat. His intention was to study at the University in Herat, both the Islamic sciences and their inner meanings. At the outset of their journey, they happened to stop in the village of Shadiman where Shaykh UbaydAllah (q) was staying. After the noon prayer they went to pay him their respects.

Shaykh UbaydAllah (q) took great interest in Muhammad (q) and questioned him closely as to the purpose of his journey and his goal in pursuing knowledge. He took him by the hand and led him into the garden out of sight of the others. As soon as their hands touched, Muhammad (q) felt his sense of having a separate identity disappear. Shaykh UbaydAllah (q) answered all his inner questions, showing that he knew Muhammad (q) better than Muhammad (q) knew himself. Then Shaykh UbaydAllah (q) presented him to each of the Grandshaykhs of the Golden Chain. Muhammad (q) was drawn to Shaykh UbaydAllah (q) in his heart but still his mind was set on traveling to Herat.

Shaykh UbaydAllah (q) counseled him to leave his academic studies and to stay and study with him. He gave him a copy of his writings saying that they contained within them all he needed to know. Then he gave him a letter of introduction to a friend in Bukhara who would help him on his way. Muhammad (q) was overwhelmed with the kindness of Shaykh UbaydAllah (q) but still his intention to leave remained firm.

Shaykh UbaydAllah (q) read him a passage from his writings which said: The true nature of religion lies in reverence for God, humbleness before Him, asking for His help, and seeking His forgiveness. These qualities arise in the heart by contemplating Allah's Glorious Majesty and Greatness. Success in reaching this goal depends on love, love depends on obedience to the Prophet (sas), and obedience depends on learning to obey.

Still Muhammad (q) was determined to continue on in his search for knowledge. With the Shaykh's reluctant permission, Muhammad (q) and his friend took their leave and set out on the road to Bukhara. From then on they had nothing but difficulty. It took them many months to reach Bukhara because Muhammad's (q) donkey was so slow they had to stop and rest every couple of miles. Eventually he had to trade in his donkey for another. The new one was hardly faster than the first one. Six times he traded in his donkey for another and each one was as weak and slow as the one before. Finally Muhammad (q) and his friend reached Bukhara. They were welcomed and generously hosted at the house of Shaykh UbaydAllah's (q) friend.

As they were about to continue on their journey to Herat, Muhammad (q) developed trouble with his eyes. They became so infected he could hardly see. When they finally cleared up and he again intended to leave for Herat he came down with a very high fever. At this point he felt in his heart that if he continued on to Herat he might actually die. He decided to return to Shadiman and to Shaykh UbaydAllah (q).

On his return journey it occurred to him to pay a visit to another well-known shaykh. He left his donkey with all his baggage at the inn where he was staying and set off on foot in the direction of the shaykh's house. A man came running after him shouting. The donkey he had left safely stabled at the inn had just disappeared. It was gone without a trace. Muhammad (q) knew immediately that this must be another sign from Shaykh UbaydAllah (q). After all the Shaykh's attention and advice, Muhammad (q) had still delayed in obeying what his heart was telling him. Instead of going directly to UbaydAllah (q) he was wasting time visiting someone else.

Muhammad (q) turned around in the direction of the inn. He put all other things in this world behind him and made the firm intention to return directly to Shaykh UbaydAllah (q).

As soon as he reached the inn his donkey with its saddlebags filled with books mysteriously reappeared. Shaykh Muhammad (q) wasted no more time but set off immediately for the mosque of Shaykh UbaydAllah (q).

After this prolonged lesson in obedience to the Shaykh, Muhammad (q) never once left his side. He served him until Shaykh UbaydAllah (q) died in 896 AH / 1490 CE. During that time, when Shaykh UbaydAllah (q) gave a lecture he usually addressed it directly to Shaykh Muhammad (q). He knew that Shaykh Muhammad (q) would most probably understand and if he did not, he would accept humbly without questioning. Shaykh Muhammad (q) witnessed the many miracles of Shaykh UbaydAllah (q), and after his death he wrote a now famous book about him. He inherited the light and the secret and continued to guide the seekers who came to him.

Shaykh Muhammad (q) died on the day of Mawlid, in 936 AH / 1529 CE in Samarkand. He passed the secret of the Golden Chain to Darwish Muhammad (q).

May Allah bless an-Nabi (sas), as-Siddiq (ra), Salman (ra), Qasim (ra), Jafar (ra), Tayfur (q), Abul Hasan (q), Abu Ali (q), Yusuf (q), Abul Abbas al-Khidr (as), Abdul Khaliq (q), Arif (q), Mahmoud (q), Ali (q), Muhammad Baba as-Samasi (q), Sayyid Amir Kulal (q), Shah Bahauddin an-Naqshband (q), Alauddin (q), Ya'qub (q), UbaydAllah (q), and Muhammad az-Zahid (q).

116 Links of Light: The Golden Chain

22
Darwish Muhammmad (q)

Darwish Muhammad (q) was the nephew of Muhammad az-Zahid (q) who was both his uncle and his shaykh. He grew up in Shaykh Muhammad's (q) house, in the middle of the dhikr circle. His uncle educated him carefully in all things, both religious and spiritual.

One day when he had grown into a young man, as he passed to kiss his uncle's hand after a lecture, Muhammad az-Zahid (q) said to him quietly, "Go climb that mountain over there and wait for me to come." Darwish Muhammad (q) followed the directions of his shaykh immediately. He did not ask himself, "Why am I being ordered up the mountain? What will I do there? How long will I have to wait?" He put all these doubts aside and moved quickly to obey his shaykh

He climbed to the top of the mountain, prayed the noontime prayer and waited. His uncle did not come. He prayed the late afternoon prayer and waited. His uncle was still nowhere in sight. His ego began to whisper inside his head, "Your shaykh is never coming. Maybe he forgot. You should go down the mountain and return to him." His true self answered his ego, "O Darwish Muhammad, trust that your shaykh will do what he said. Nothing he says is without purpose. He will not forget. Be patient and wait for him here on the mountain."

He prayed the sunset prayer and waited. The shaykh did not come. Night descended and it was very cold on the mountain. He prayed the night prayer and waited but still the shaykh did not come. He began to do dhikr, *La ilaha illa Allah*. He repeated this until it warmed every part of his body and soul. He did not sleep. In the morning he prayed the morning prayer but still his shaykh did not come.

He was hungry. He found some trees with fruit still on them and he ate. He continued to wait for Muhammad az-Zahid (q) to arrive. That day passed and the next day. Darwish Muhammad (q) answered the doubting voice in his mind by saying "If my shaykh is a real shaykh he knows me and my situation. My path can only be to obey him."

A week went by, then a month. Still the shaykh did not come. Darwish Muhammad (q) waited. His prayers and his dhikr were his only companions. He continued in this way until the power of *La ilaha illa Allah* began to attract the wild animals. The deer and the foxes, the falcons and the doves, gathered around him in peace to join in remembrance of their Creator, Allah Almighty.

Winter came. It began to snow. Still the shaykh did not come. Darwish Muhammad (q) could find no more fruit or berries. He began to strip the bark off the trees to eat. He dug up roots from the frozen ground. The deer came to nuzzle him and keep him warm. The mother deer allowed him to drink her sweet milk. He began to experience many visions and miracles. He was no longer alone on the mountain. Khidr (as) came to teach him spiritual wisdom. As he patiently waited on his desolate mountaintop the whole world came to him.

A year passed and then another year and another. He waited but still the shaykh did not come. For seven years Darwish Muhammad (q) remained in a state of expectation and patient waiting. One day Darwish Muhammad (q) started to smell a beautiful fragrant perfume. He recognized it as the spiritual scent of his shaykh, Muhammad az-Zahid (q). It kept coming closer and closer. His shaykh was finally climbing up the mountain. Beside himself with joy, he began to run down the path directly towards the source of the beautiful perfume. A wild figure, covered in long hair and followed by a swarm of wild animals, Darwish Muhammad (q) threw himself at the feet of his beloved shaykh. He kissed the hands and feet of Muhammad az-Zahid (q), while his heart soared with love.

Shaykh Muhammad az-Zahid (q) laughed and at that moment poured the lights and secrets of the Golden Chain into the heart of Darwish Muhammad (q). Darwish Muhammad

(q) returned to the village and married and had a family. Years later, after his shaykh had died, Darwish Muhammad (q) took over the teaching of the students. He led them steadily towards the light. The school and mosque of his uncle were always full of visitors and seekers. He mended hearts that were broken and restored hearts that had become tired and weak. He was the blessing of his time and the heart of guidance.

Darwish Muhammad (q) died on the nineteenth of the month of *Muharram*, in the year 970 AH / 1562 CE. He passed the light and the secret of the Golden Chain to his own son, Muhammad al-Amkanaki (q).

May Allah bless an-Nabi (sas), as-Siddiq (ra), Salman (ra), Qasim (ra) Jafar (ra), Tayfur (q), Abul Hasan (q), Abu Ali (q), Yusuf (q), Abul Abbas al-Khidr (as), Abdul Khaliq (q), Arif (q), Mahmoud (q), Ali (q), Muhammad Baba as-Samasi (q), Sayyid Amir Kulal (q), Shah Bahauddin an-Naqshband (q), Alauddin (q), Ya'qub (q), UbaydAllah (q), Muhammad az-Zahid (q), and Darwish Muhammad (q).

120 Links of Light: The Golden Chain

23
Muhammad al-Amkanaki (q)

Shaykh Muhammad al-Amkanaki (q) was born in the town of Amkana, which lies on the outskirts of Bukhara. His name means Muhammad of Amkana. His father was Shaykh Darwish Muhammad (q) and his great uncle was the Grandshaykh of the Golden Chain, Muhammad az-Zahid (q). He was raised in the house of his great uncle and educated by him until his death. His father then continued to guide him lovingly towards the highest truths.

From childhood he was protected from bad actions and unkind thoughts. He saw every little thing in the world around him as a reflection and reminder of God Almighty. Whenever he saw anything good in someone he learned how to be like that too. Any bad action, however small, once he noticed it he never did again. Any high spiritual state he saw, he worked hard to attain. Any deep spiritual secret, entrusted to him, he securely kept. And every delicious spiritual taste, he appreciated to the fullest.

He followed his father until his light shone like the sun on a bright day or like the moon on a dark night. He spent his days trying to help people, to lift them up and enlighten their hearts. For this reason his mosque was always crowded with seekers. His reputation spread far and wide. People came from the ends of the earth to ask for his advice and his blessing.

Every single particle in this world, human or jinn, fish or animal, plant or stone, took its light from him and relied on him for spiritual support. He was the crown on the whole of God's creation.

He died in 1008 AH / 1599 CE. He passed the secrets and the lights of the Golden Chain to Muhammad al-Baqi Billah (q).

May Allah bless an-Nabi (sas), as-Siddiq (ra), Salman (ra), Qasim (ra), Jafar (ra), Tayfur (q), Abul Hasan (q), Abu Ali (q), Yusuf (q), Abul Abbas al-Khidr (as), Abdul Khaliq (q), Arif (q), Mahmoud (q), Ali (q), Muhammad Baba as-Samasi (q), Sayyid Amir Kulal (q), Shah Bahauddin an-Naqshband (q), Alauddin (q), Ya'qub (q), UbaydAllah (q), Muhammad az-Zahid (q), Darwish Muhammad (q), and Muhammad al-Amkanaki (q).

124 Links of Light: The Golden Chain

24
Muhammad al-Baqi Billah (q)

Shaykh Muhammad al-Baqi Billah (q) was born in 972 AH / 1564 CE in the city of Kabul, in what is now Afghanistan but was at that time a province of the Sultanate of India. His father was a very famous judge named Qadi Abdus-Salam.

Shaykh Muhammad (q) was educated by his father in all things that related to religion. Then as a young man he was sent to India on business. In India the taste for spiritual knowledge awoke inside of him and he lost all interest in business and worldly things. He kept company only with the masters and saints until, in a short time, he became like them. He was a master of both oceans of knowledge, worldly knowledge and heavenly knowledge. In addition, Allah gave him power over both the world of jinn and the world of man.

His thirst for knowledge was so intense that he began to search for it wherever in the world he could find it. He started to travel. For many years he moved constantly from place to place always looking for the perfect shaykh. He went beyond the borders of India until he finally reached the city of Bukhara.

In Bukhara he went to pay his respects to a shaykh about whom he had heard many wonderful things, Shaykh Muhammad al-Amkanaki (q). He took his hand and connected his heart to the heart of the shaykh. In a very short time his heart opened to the secrets that most seekers only receive after a lifetime of work. After making this connection he also began to be taught by the Shaykhs of the Golden Chain who had already left this world. In particular he received guidance from UbaydAllah al-Ahrar (q). For this reason Shaykh Muhammad (q) is also called *Uwaysi*.

After some time he was ordered by his shaykh, Muhammad al-Amkanaki (q), to return to India and establish a teaching center. In India he would find the one who would become his closest follower and eventually, his successor. This student would come to be the greatest saint of his time, the pole around which the whole world turns, the reviver of the religion.

So although he found it very painful to leave the shaykh he had been searching for for so long, Muhammad al-Baqi (q) returned to India and settled down in the city of Delhi. After a little while it became obvious that any person who came to Muhammad al-Baqi (q), even just one time, and sat with him in dhikr, would reach the highest states of spiritual awareness. His name and his way became famous all over India and people traveled long distances just to kiss his hand and sit in his company. Even people of other religions began to recognize and appreciate his spiritual powers. Many of them came to Islam through their love for him. The entire city of Delhi was filled with lights and peace through his blessed influence.

Muhammad al-Baqi Billah (q) died on Wednesday the fourteenth of the month of *Jumada al-Akhir* in the year 1014 AH / 1605 CE. He was only forty years old at the time of his death. He is buried on the west side of the city of Delhi. Before he died he passed the secret and the light of the Golden Chain to his closest follower, Ahmad al-Faruqi (q), the one forseen by Shaykh Muhammad al-Amkanaki (q).

May Allah bless an-Nabi (sas), as-Siddiq (ra), Salman (ra), Qasim (ra), Jafar (ra), Tayfur (q), Abul Hasan (q), Abu Ali (q), Yusuf (q), Abul Abbas al-Khidr (as), Abdul Khaliq (q), Arif (q), Mahmoud (q), Ali (q), Muhammad Baba as-Samasi (q), Sayyid Amir Kulal (q), Shah Bahauddin an-Naqshband (q), Alauddin (q), Ya'qub (q), UbaydAllah (q), Muhammad az-Zahid (q), Darwish Muhammad (q), Muhammad al-Amkanaki (q), and Muhammad al-Baqi (q).

25
Ahmad al-Faruqi as-Sirhindi (q)

Shaykh Ahmad (q) was born on the day of *Ashura*, the tenth of the month of Muharram, in the year 971 AH / 1564 CE. He was born in the town of Sirhind, near the city of Lahore, in what is now Pakistan but was then part of India. His father was a direct descendant of Umar al-Faruq (ra), the close Companion of the Prophet Muhammad (sas) and the second of the rightly guided leaders of the Muslims.

By the young age of seventeen Shaykh Ahmad (q) was already recognized in spiritual circles as being remarkable. Although he was very accomplished and had already been given authority by three shaykhs of three different spiritual ways to train students, he still felt something was missing. He kept searching until one day he traveled to Delhi and found Shaykh Muhammad al-Baqi Billah (q). Shaykh Muhammad (q) had been ordered many years before, by his own shaykh, Muhammad al-Amkanaki (q), to leave Bukhara and return to India to await the great saint for whom the whole world also waited. Muhammad al-Baqi (q) recognized immediately that Shaykh Ahmad (q) was the one for whom he had been told to wait.

Every hundred years Allah sends a saint into the world, whose spiritual powers renew and refresh the religion. Every thousand years, however, Allah sends a saint who revives the religion on an even greater scale. Over the years some of the wisdoms brought by the Prophet (sas) and some of the practices he taught are forgotten or neglected. What has been forgotten this saint recalls. What has been twisted he straightens. What has been abandoned he rescues. He has the power to make everything as new and fresh and beautiful as it was when it was first revealed. Ahmad al-Faruqi (q) was the Reviver of the Millenium, the first thousand years since the coming of Islam, 1000 AH. It is believed that the Prophet (sas) himself predicted the coming of Shaykh Ahmad (q), as recorded in the Hadith.

Muhammad al-Baqi (q) accepted Shaykh Ahmad (q) immediately and opened his heart to the luminous secrets of the Golden Chain. Shaykh Ahmad (q) was taken on a journey through the whole of creation including the seven heavens. He was taken up to the Throne of Allah Almighty. Below him he saw the station of many shaykhs. Above him he saw the station of Shah Naqshband (q) and above that, on one side the station of the Prophets (ahums) and, on the other side, the exalted station of an-Nabi Muhammad (sas). He was taken to visit them all.

Many of these shaykhs who had already died became his teachers in the spiritual realms. Alauddin al-Attar (q) in particular became his close companion. Even Sayyidina Khidr (as) served as his guide. He was *Uwaysi* because he was taught through the direct connection of his heart to the heart of the Prophet (sas) himself.

Shaykh Ahmad (q) was taken to very high and exalted spiritual stations. Then Allah ordered him to return to lead an ordinary life among the people of this world. Remaining in direct connection with his Lord while going about his daily business, he set an example that all people can try to follow.

Shaykh Ahmad (q) was not an ordinary man, however. Allah gave him many extraordinary powers. He was able to heal the sick and to make the blind see again. He said that if his gaze even happened to fall on a dead tree, it would immediately begin to sprout green leaves.

He was also able to be in more than one place at the same time. One night in the fasting month of Ramadan he received ten different invitations to break fast. Much to everyone's surprise, he accepted all ten of the invitations. When the time arrived for breaking fast everyone waited to see which one of the ten hosts would be honored by the presence of the shaykh. To their great surprise Shaykh Ahmad (q) was seen by each of the ten, sitting as an honored guest in his home, eating and drinking.

At one point the advisors of the King became concerned that Shaykh Ahmad (q) had too much power over the people and might become a threat to the authority of the King himself. They advised the King to put Shaykh Ahmad (q) in jail for a while in order to question him and observe his reactions. He was put in a high security cell surrounded by guards, day and night. He stayed quietly, studying the Quran, praying and doing dhikr. He used the time as a religious seclusion and to be of service to the men who kept him prisoner.

Every Friday, no matter how many soldiers were placed around his cell to keep watch, Shaykh Ahmad (q) would disappear for a few hours. He would be seen at the central mosque, joining the people of the city in the required Friday congregational prayer. No matter what his jailors did, Shaykh Ahmad (q) always walked free for a few hours on Friday. After three years the government finally realized that if Shaykh Ahmad (q) wanted, by Allah's permission, he could walk free at any time. They had no control over him. So they let him go.

The King and his advisors eventually took the hand of Shaykh Ahmad (q). All of India began to glow with his beauty and light. He used to say that he had been taken to the presence of Allah and then brought back so that he could serve as a connection between heaven and earth, in much the same way that a thread rises to pass through the eye of a needle and then returns to where it started to have both ends knotted together. Beginning and ending, needle and thread, all are connected into one. Anyone attached to that thread, like a bead on a string, also necessarily becomes one with them. In this way Shaykh Ahmad (q) strung the whole of creation together as one, in the worship of their Lord.

Shaykh Ahmad al-Faruqi (q) left us many of his books in which he recorded his extraordinary experiences and insights. He died at the age of 63, (the same age as the Prophet (sas) had been at his death), on the seventeenth of *Safar* in the year 1034 AH / 1624 CE. He was buried in the city in which he was born, Sirhind. He passed the secrets and the lights of the Golden Chain to his son, Muhammad Ma'sum (q).

May Allah bless, an-Nabi (sas), as-Siddiq (ra), Salman (ra), Qasim (ra), Jafar (ra), Tayfur (q), Abul Hasan (q), Abu Ali (q), Yusuf (q), Abul Abbas al-Khidr (as), Abdul Khaliq (q), Arif (q), Mahmoud (q), Ali (q), Muhammad Baba as-Samasi (q), Sayyid Amir Kulal (q), Shah Bahauddin an-Naqshband (q), Alauddin (q), Ya'qub (q), UbaydAllah (q), Muhammad az-Zahid (q), Darwish Muhammad (q), Muhammad al-Amkanaki (q), Muhammad al-Baqi (q), and Ahmad al-Faruqi (q).

134   Links of Light: The Golden Chain

26

Muhammad Ma'sum (q)

Shaykh Muhammad Ma'sum (q) was born in the year 1007 AH / 1599 CE. His father was Shaykh Ahmad al-Faruqi (q). He grew up under his father's careful watch, surrounded by the remembrance of God, and with his feet securely planted on the Naqshbandi Way.

He was clearly seen to be a saint even as a baby. He fasted his first Ramadan by refusing to drink his mother's milk during the day, nursing only at night. By the age of three he was speaking spiritual truths, declaring his closeness to God and all of His creation. He was in harmony with the heavens and the earth. At the age of six he memorized the whole of the Quran in only three months. At the age of seventeen he was a recognized scholar of Islamic law, Hadith and legal judgments. He was considered to be the greatest scholar of his time before he was twenty. But his true greatness lay in the light that filled his knowing heart.

At the age of twenty-six he lost his loving father and shaykh. Shaykh Ahmad as-Sirhindi (q) died leaving Muhammad Ma'sum (q) in charge of the teaching of those who came from all over the world looking for a way to please God. Shaykh Ahmad (q) said before he died, "I have poured into my son, Muhammad Ma'sum (q), everything I have been given. He was made from the clay that was left over from making me. I was made from the clay that was left over from making the Prophet (sas)."

Shaykh Muhammad Ma'sum (q) was a miracle of God's Miracles, and a light given to all of humanity. It is said that nine hundred thousand (900,000) people took his hand and were introduced to the Naqshbandi Way. He had seven thousand (7,000) deputies to help him in teaching and advising all of these followers. Each one of these helpers was a saint in his own right. It is also said that it was possible, by sitting with him for just one week, to be taken to the highest stations.

When he visited Mecca, the Ka'aba rose to greet him, and hugged and kissed him with great emotion. When he went to Madina to pay his respects at the grave of the Prophet (sas), the Prophet (sas) rose from his grave and hugged him while he poured knowledge and light into his open heart. At this time he came to understand that all of creation, from the tiniest ant on the face of the earth to the farthest star in the vast expanse of the heavens, is in need of the beloved Prophet (sas). An-Nabi Muhammad (sas) is truly the center of all light that shines in every single atom of creation, no matter how big or how tiny.

He performed many miraculous deeds in the fulfillment of his duty to take care of those entrusted to him. He healed those who were sick. He restored the sight of those who were blind. He helped those who were in need.

Once he was sitting inside his mosque, surrounded by his companions. All of a sudden they began to notice that the sleeves of his coat were drenched with water. Streams of water were running off his hands and forearms, but there was no source of water anywhere nearby. His companions, in alarm, asked Shaykh Muhammad Ma'sum (q) what had happened. He answered that one of his followers was traveling on a ship faraway. All of a sudden a storm had arisen and huge waves were battering the small ship. The follower of Shaykh Muhammad (q) was washed over the side of the boat into the raging sea. He called out in his desperate fear, "O my Shaykh, help me!" Shaykh Muhammad Ma'sum (q), from his spot in the mosque, reached his hands through time and space into the stormy waters and pulled his follower to safety. It was for this reason that his sleeves and hands were drenched with seawater.

His companions in the mosque noted down the time and the day of this strange occurrence. Many months later a traveler arrived at the mosque and related a story about how he had been washed into the sea and had seen the strong arms of Shaykh Muhammad

Ma'sum (q) reach out of the air and pull him to safety. It had been exactly at the time and on the day the companions in the mosque had witnessed the Shaykh's hands dripping with water.

Shaykh Muhammad Ma'sum (q) continued his father's work until India glowed with the light and the love of God. He died on the ninth of *Rabi al-Awwal* in the year 1079 AH/ 1668 CE. He passed the secret and the light of the Golden Chain to his own son, Muhammad Sayfuddin al-Faruqi al-Mujaddidi (q).

May Allah bless, an-Nabi (sas), as-Siddiq (ra), Salman (ra), Qasim (ra), Jafar (ra), Tayfur (q), Abul Hasan (q), Abu Ali (q), Yusuf (q), Abul Abbas al-Khidr (as), Abdul Khaliq (q), Arif (q), Mahmoud (q), Ali (q), Muhammad Baba as-Samasi (q), Sayyid Amir Kulal (q), Shah Bahauddin an-Naqshband (q), Alauddin (q), Ya'qub (q), UbaydAllah (q), Muhammad az-Zahid (q), Darwish Muhammad (q), Muhammad al-Amkanaki (q), Muhammad al-Baqi (q), Ahmad al-Faruqi (q), and Muhammad Ma'sum (q).

138 Links of Light: The Golden Chain

27

Muhammad Sayfuddin (q)

Shaykh Muhammad Sayfuddin (q) was born in the year 1055 AH / 1645 CE in Sirhind. He was the son of Muhammad Ma'sum (q) and the grandson of Ahmad al-Faruqi (q). He inherited a deep spiritual nature from both. His father introduced him to the Shaykhs of the Golden Chain and to the Prophets. He followed in the footsteps of those who had come before him until he sat on the throne of guidance.

During his father's lifetime he served as his deputy. His house became a light for the scholars of religion. They were drawn to him like moths to a lamp, attracted from all over the world. He taught both beginners and those far along on the path. It is said that he taught the knowledge of taste. He led each seeker to such a real experience of God that they knew with their heart, mind, and body that they had actually tasted and touched the Truth.

On the orders of his father, Shaykh Muhammad Sayfuddin (q) moved to the city of Delhi, the capitol of the Sultanate of India. The Sultan, Muhammad Alamgir, took his hand and sat humbly at his feet in order to gain knowledge. As a result all the members of the royal court, the ministers and the princes, also became followers of Shaykh Sayfuddin (q). In a short time the whole Sultanate of India accepted Sayfuddin (q) as their shaykh. When he entered the palace all the princes and courtiers rose to their feet in respect.

Allah loves and supports those who love and support His beloved ones. Because of the Sultan's love for Shaykh Sayfuddin (q) Allah blessed the Sultan with success in all his efforts. Whenever he could the Sultan kept company with the Shaykh. During the long hours of the night the Sultan prayed and studied the Quran under his direction. With the Shaykh's help the Sultan memorized the whole of the Quran.

During the day the Sultan sat on the throne and, under Shaykh Sayfuddin's (q) direction, ruled with justice and mercy. By means of his influence over the Sultan, Shaykh Sayfuddin (q) worked to eliminate all forms of misery and tyranny from the kingdom. The true nature of Islam shone in every corner of the kingdom. There was peace and unity, appreciation for beauty and knowledge, respect for God's creation, and reverence for God Himself.

Every day at least six thousand (6,000) people gathered at the house of the Shaykh to listen to his lectures and take blessing from his company. The Shaykh welcomed them all. He fed them and found places for them to sleep while they were his guests. He never turned anyone away.

One day Shaykh Sayfuddin (q) heard the sound of someone playing the reed flute. He immediately lost consciousness and collapsed on the ground. His followers could not understand what had happened and they were afraid for his safety. When he awoke he scolded them. How was it possible that they did not also faint when they heard the longing and love carried on the sound of the flute? Shaykh Sayfuddin (q) experienced all beauty as a direct call from Allah to come into His Divine Presence. So at the sound of the flute Shaykh Sayfuddin (q) had immediately answered Allah's call. He left everything in this world behind and went directly to God. This is the true meaning of the spiritual ability to taste.

When Shaykh Muhammad Sayfuddin (q) died in 1095 AH / 1684 CE he was buried, with much grieving and royal ceremony, next to his father and grandfather in Sirhind. He passed the secret and the light of the Golden Chain to Nur Muhammad al-Badawani (q).

May Allah bless, an-Nabi (sas), Siddiq (ra), Salman (ra), Qasim (ra), Jafar (ra), Tayfur (q), Abul Hasan (q), Abu Ali, (q), Yusuf (q), Abul Abbas al-Khidr (as), Abdul Khaliq (q), Arif (q), Mahmoud (q), Ali (q), Muhammad Baba as-Samasi (q), Sayyid Amir Kulal (q), Shah Bahauddin an-Naqshband (q), Alauddin (q), Ya'qub (q), UbaydAllah (q), Muhammad az-Zahid (q), Darwish Muhammad (q), Muhammad al-Amkanaki (q), Muhammad al-Baqi (q), Ahmad al-Faruqi (q), Muhammad Ma'sum (q), and Sayfuddin (q).

142 Links of Light: The Golden Chain

28

Nur Muhammad al-Badawani (q)

Shaykh Nur Muhammad (q) was born in India in 1075 AH / 1664 CE. A descendant of the Prophet Muhammad (sas), he was born into a household that already followed the Naqshbandi Way. His father was a follower of Shaykh Sayfuddin (q) and he introduced his son at an early age. Shaykh Nur Muhammad (q) drank from the fountain of knowledge of the Shaykhs of the Golden Chain until he became an ocean of light. Even as a child people came from all over India to sit with him and receive his blessing.

As a young man he was totally unconcerned about how he appeared to others. He paid no attention to how he dressed or where he slept or what was going on around him. As long as it was according to the practice of the Prophet (sas) he was content. He did not notice if it was winter or summer. He did not notice if there was war or peace. He did not notice if the people were happy or sad. He wanted nothing and was not even aware that there might be something to want. When it came time for prayer he became, for that brief time, aware of his self and his condition. He performed the prescribed prayers and all the extra prayers of the Prophet (sas) in complete awareness. Then he resumed his remembrance and contemplation of his Lord and became again lost to his self.

He ate only bread that he had ground, kneaded, and baked with his own hands. Even of this bread he ate very little. Never in his whole life did he think or worry about earning a living or from where his next meal would come. For fifteen (15) years he did only what he needed to do to stay alive. He sat at the feet of Shaykh Sayfuddin (q) and devoted himself entirely to dhikr, study, and comtemplation of the wonders of Allah.

He pursued all forms of knowledge, but his particular interest was the character and morals of the Prophet Muhammad (sas). He read all the books he could find. He consulted all the learned men, those in his city and those passing through. Everything he learned he applied to himself and tried to implement in his own life. He became a living, breathing reflection of the Prophet Muhammad (sas). He walked as he (sas) walked. He dressed as he (sas) dressed. He ate as he (sas) ate. One day, by mistake, he entered the bathroom with his right foot. It was the practice of the Prophet (sas), on entering any unclean place, to put his left foot first. As a consequence of this one small misstep, which represented a single moment of heedlessness, Shaykh Nur Muhammad (q) was given to endure much stomach pain, and for three days was unable to use the bathroom at all.

To those who knew him Shaykh Nur Muhammad (q) was a miracle of God's miracles. His sensitivity, his knowledge, his humility, his perfect following of the Prophet (sas), served as clear proof of God's power and generosity. Without Allah's help no ordinary person could have followed in the footsteps of the Prophet (sas) with such perfection and attention to detail.

After thirty years Shaykh Nur Muhammmad (q) became extremely sensitive to anything not in accordance with the Sunnah of the Prophet (sas). If he read a book he could feel the negative influence of the character of the author. When he met a student he immediately sensed any improper thing the student might have seen or done on his way to the mosque. If the student had merely been in the company of someone else who had done something contrary to the Sunnah of the Prophet (sas) he could sense it. Shaykh Nur Muhammad (q) could see with the eyes of his heart better than most people can see with the eyes of their head.

Shaykh Nur Muhammad (q) died in the year 1135 AH / 1722 CE. He passed the secret of the Golden Chain to his successor, Shaykh Shamsuddin Habib-Allah Jan-i-Janan al-Mazhar (q).

May Allah bless, an-Nabi (sas), Siddiq (ra), Salman (ra), Qasim (ra), Jafar (ra), Tayfur (q), Abul Hasan (q), Abu Ali (q), Yusuf (q), Abul Abbas al-Khidr (as), Abdul Khaliq (q), Arif (q), Mahmoud (q), Ali (q), Muhammad Baba as-Samasi (q), Sayyid Amir Kulal (q), Shah Bahauddin an-Naqshband (q), Alauddin (q), Ya'qub (q), UbaydAllah (q), Muhammad az-Zahid (q), Darwish Muhammad (q), Muhammad al-Amkanaki (q), Muhammad al-Baqi (q), Ahmad al-Faruqi (q), Muhammad Ma'sum (q), Sayfuddin (q), and Nur Muhammad (q).

146 Links of Light: The Golden Chain

29 Shamsuddin Habib Allah (q)

Shaykh Shamsuddin Habib Allah Jan-i-Janan al-Mazhar (q) was born in India in 1113 AH / 1701 CE. His name, Habib Allah, is one of the many names of the Prophet Muhammmad (sas) and it means, beloved of God. Even in childhood the light of Muhammad (sas) could be clearly seen, shining from his forhead. He was so handsome that he was compared to the Prophet Muhammad (sas) and the Prophet Yusuf (as), the two most beautiful of all the prophets. It is said that most of the beauty that Allah created for the entire universe was given to the Prophet Yusuf (as).

The Prophet Muhammad (sas) with his Companions, in particular Abu Bakr as-Siddiq (ra), would visit him regularly. When Shaykh Habib Allah (q) was nine years old the Prophet Ibrahim (as) appeared to him and gave him special powers.

His father sent him to many famous scholars to learn the religious sciences, Quran, and Hadith. But his heart was always drawn to the spiritual wisdom he found when sitting with Shaykh Nur Muhammad al-Badawani (q). Shaykh Nur Muhammad (q) opened the eyes of his heart and took him on many spiritual journeys. What Shaykh Habib Allah (q) witnessed during these experiences caused such astonishment and awe in him that often he would faint. Shaykh Nur Muhammad (q) would patiently wait for him to awake and then take him to higher and even higher stations. All the Shaykhs of the Naqshbandi order would appear to Shaykh Habib Allah (q) and give him spiritual knowledge, expecially Shaykh Ahmad al-Faruqi (q).

Shaykh Habib Allah (q) kept constant company with Shaykh Nur Muhammad (q) and served him with truthfulness and deep sincerity. After some years, he was ordered to go into seclusion. Sometimes in the jungle, sometimes in the desert, he was sent to pray and do dhikr by himself for many months at a time. Once when he returned he happened to see his reflection in a mirror. He no longer saw his own face but he saw only the face of his Shaykh, Nur Muhammad (q), looking back at him. Shaykh Habib Allah had completely disappeared. He had become one with his Shaykh.

After Shaykh Nur Muhammad (q) died, Shaykh Habib Allah (q) continued to keep company with him by staying by the side of his grave and Shaykh Nur Muhammad (q) continued to teach him. After two years, however, he was ordered to find and follow a living shaykh. For twenty years Shaykh Habib Allah (q) sat with many famous shaykhs and masters, learning from each of them, until he was considered to be the spiritual center of the universe. His previous teachers then took his hand and became his followers. He said, "This whole world and the entire universe that surrounds it, are in my hand. I can see every thing that is in them, just as clearly as I can see my own hand."

One time he set out on a journey with some of his followers. They took with them no food, or water, or provisions of any kind. Every day, from out of nowhere, tables of food would appear for them to eat. One day a terrible storm arose and with it a freezing wind. It tore through everything in its path. The followers of the Shaykh huddled together, shivering and shaking in the ice and rain. They felt they would surely die in that freezing wasteland. Shaykh Habib Allah (q) raised his hands and asked, "O Allah, make it around us without being upon us." Immediately the clouds lifted from over them. The freezing rain withdrew. Just one mile away the rain, wind, and hail continued to batter the land, but over and around the Shaykh the wind became soft and gentle. The temperature grew warmer and in this protected space they continued on their journey.

When he became eighty years old Shaykh Habib Allah (q) began to feel sad that he still continued to live in this world. He longed for the company of his Lord. He spent more and more of his time in intense worship and prayer. The spiritual light that radiated from his beautiful face attracted more and more people. Each day three thousand (3,000) new people would come to visit him. He would not let any one of them leave without meeting him.

Finally he became so exhausted that he scheduled only two times during the day to sit with people.

He told his followers that everything he had wished for in this life, Allah had given him except for one thing. His last wish was to return to Allah as described in the Holy Quran, as a martyr who has earned eternal life. (A martyr is a person whose death occurs only because he has followed in the Way of Allah, standing up for Truth, Justice, and Righteousness.)

On Wednesday, the seventh of the month of Muharram, 1195 AH / 1781 CE, three men came to visit Shaykh Habib Allah (q). The first man asked him if he was Jan-i-Janan Habib Allah (q), the one they call Shaykh? When he answered that indeed he was, they stabbed him with their knives. He fell to the ground, gravely wounded. His followers were horrified and desperate. The King sent his own private doctor to try to heal the wound. Shaykh Habib Allah (q), however, was calm and content. He sent the doctor back to the King. He had no need of him. He forgave the ones who stabbed him because, he said, they had only come as an answer to his prayer to die as a martyr.

On Friday he recited *Surat Yasin* all day until sunset. Then, in fulfillment of his last wish, his soul left his body. He returned to his Lord, a martyr, on the holy day of the tenth of Muharram 1195 AH/ 1781 CE. He passed the secret of the Golden Chain to his successor, Shaykh AbdAllah ad-Dahlawi (q).

May Allah bless, an-Nabi (sas), Siddiq (ra), Salman (ra), Qasim (ra), Jafar (ra), Tayfur (q), Abul Hasan (q), Abu Ali (q), Yusuf (q), Abul Abbas al-Khidr (as), Abdul Khaliq (q), Arif (q), Mahmoud (q), Ali (q), Muhammad Baba as-Samasi (q), Sayyid Amir Kulal (q), Shah Bahauddin an-Naqshband (q), Alauddin (q), Ya'qub (q), UbaydAllah (q), Muhammad az-Zahid (q), Darwish Muhammad (q), Muhammad al-Amkanaki (q), Muhammad al-Baqi (q), Ahmad al-Faruqi (q), Muhammad Ma'sum (q), Sayfuddin (q), Nur Muhammad (q), and Habib Allah (q).

152 Links of Light: The Golden Chain

30
Abdallah ad-Dahlawi, Shah Ghulam Ali (q)

Shaykh AbdAllah (q) was born in 1158 AH / 1745 CE in the village of Bitala in the Punjab area of India. He was a descendant of the noble family of the Prophet Muhammad (sas). Before he was born, his father saw Sayyidina Ali (as), the cousin and son-in-law of the Prophet (sas), in a dream. Sayyidina Ali (as) told him that he would have a saintly son and that he should name the boy after him. Later when his mother was pregnant, both she and his father had an identical dream. They each dreamed that the Prophet (sas) himself told them to name their son AbdAllah. Because obedience to the Prophet's (sas) order comes first, when their child was born they named him AbdAllah Shah Ghulam Ali (q). His name means, Servant of God, King, servant of Ali.

As a child he memorized the entire Quran in only one month's time. Later he studied the Islamic sciences, the meaning of the Quran, and the Hadith, under many famous scholars. As a young man he began to spend a lot of time alone in the desert. He devoted himself to the worship of God, without care for material things. He paid no attention to what he was wearing or even if he had food or water. His dhikr, his remembrance of God, was continuous, and unbroken by any other thought or activity.

At the age of twenty-two he traveled to Delhi and found Shaykh Jan-i-Janan Habib Allah (q). He immediately asked to take initiation and become his student. After a short time he was accepted. For fifteen years Shaykh AbdAllah (q) served Shaykh Habib Allah (q). He lived on a little money that he got by renting out a piece of land he had inherited. Eventually he gave this land away in charity in order to please Allah and to be completely reliant on Him. After this he lived in a tiny shack with only a thin mat for a bed and a hard pillow on which to rest his head.

This hardship took its toll and he became sick and weak. One day he decided to lock his door and not to open it again until he received help from Allah. He would either live without food or die, whatever Allah willed. He would not, however, ask for the help of anyone other than Allah.

After forty days he heard a knock at the door. "Who is it?" he asked. A voice answered, "Open the door." "I do not want to open the door" he replied weakly. "Do you need anything?" the kind voice asked. "No. I only need God, Exalted and Mighty," he answered. At that moment Shaykh AbdAllah (q) was taken into the Presence of God Himself. He stayed in that Exalted and Radiant Place for, what felt to him like, one thousand (1,000) years. After this he was returned to his small room and commanded by Allah to open the door. His kindly neighbor gave him a hot supper and continued to provide for him for the next fifty years. This is the way Allah provided for Shaykh AbdAllah (q) for the rest of his life.

Shaykh AbdAllah (q) had a special power. He was able to reach people and guide them by appearing in their dreams. People from as far away as Syria and North Africa saw him in their dreams and searched the world until they found him. His center fed two thousand (2,000) visitors every day. When his guests had spent enough time learning from him, he sent them back to their homes. In this way he had representatives all over the Muslim world.

Shaykh AbdAllah's (q) compassion and concern for others was apparent in every small detail of his life. Even in his sleep, he never stretched out his legs. He was worried that the dirty bottoms of his feet might be directed towards some unseen being and that this would be an act of disrespect. He only slept one to two hours anyway, before rising to pray the voluntary night prayers.

He always wore old clothes. If he was given new ones he would sell them and use the money to buy lots of old clothes. These he would give to the poor, saying it was better for many people to have some clothes than for one person to have fine clothes.

Since he was unconcerned about his posessions sometimes someone would steal from him. He would never expose them, or even scold them. He said it was a matter between them and their Lord. He continued to be kind to them and speak well of them. He never said negative things about anyone, not even about the actions of the King or the politicians. He did not tolerate this kind of talk among any of his followers. They spoke only about God and religion.

One year, too little rain fell in the area where he lived. The people feared that there would be no grass for their animals to eat, no water for their crops to grow, and that their wells would run dry. One very hot, dry day Shaykh AbdAllah (q) went out into the courtyard of the mosque and stood with the sun beating down. He raised his hands and prayed, saying that he would not move or seek shade until Allah sent rain to relieve the people. He had hardly finished his prayer before the clouds rolled in and it began to pour. It rained for forty days after that and the people and animals were very happy.

When the time for his death drew near, Shaykh AbdAllah (q) told his companions that he would like to die as a martyr, just as his Shaykh, Habib Allah (q), had died. However, he remembered that Allah had been angry with the murderers of His beloved, Shaykh Habib Allah (q). Allah had punished them by causing drought and famine. This had, in turn, resulted in hardship and fighting among all the people. Shaykh AbdAllah (q) could not bear the thought of anyone suffering on account of him. Therefore, he did not ask Allah for martyrdom. He asked only that Allah take him to His Divine Presence.

On the twefth day of the month of *Safar*, in the year 1241 AH / 1825 CE, Shaykh AbdAllah ad-Dahlawi (q) returned to his Lord. He was buried next to his Shaykh, Habib Allah (q), in the city of Delhi. He passed the light and the secret of the Golden Chain to his successor, Shaykh Khalid al-Baghdadi (q).

May Allah bless, an-Nabi (sas), Siddiq (ra), Salman (ra), Qasim (ra), Jafar (ra), Tayfur (q), Abul Hasan (q), Abu Ali (q), Yusuf (q), Abul Abbas al-Khidr (as), Abdul Khaliq (q), Arif (q), Mahmoud (q), Ali (q), Muhammad Baba as-Samasi (q), Sayyid Amir Kulal (q), Shah Bahauddin an-Naqshband (q), Alauddin (q), Ya'qub (q), UbaydAllah (q), Muhammad az-Zahid (q), Darwish Muhammad (q), Muhammad al-Amkanaki (q), Muhammad al-Baqi (q), Ahmad al-Faruqi (q), Muhammad Ma'sum (q), Sayfuddin (q), Nur Muhammad (q), Habib Allah (q), and AbdAllah (q).

158 Links of Light: The Golden Chain

31
Khalid al-Baghdadi (q)

In the year 1193 AH / 1779 CE, Khalid al-Baghdadi (q) was born in the small village of Karada, near the city of Sulaymaniyyah, in the country of Iraq. He was a descendant of Sayyidina Uthman (ra), the son-in-law of the Prophet (sas) and his third khalif. Shaykh Khalid (q) grew up and studied in Sulaymaniyyah where there were many famous schools and mosques. He studied with the greatest scholars of his day, mathematics, logic and philosophy, as well as Quran, Hadith and Islamic law.

Shaykh Khalid (q) became recognized as a master of Quranic recitation. There are fourteen acceptable ways to recite Quran. Each one differs slightly from the other, in the length that the vowels are held, in the exact pronounciation of some letters, or in the places where it is permitted to stop and take a breath. Not only did Shaykh Khalid (q) know the whole Quran, but he had mastered each of these fourteen variations. It was as if he knew fourteen Qurans.

He moved to the capital city of Baghdad and continued to study there. He became a master of all the modern sciences, engineering, astronomy, and chemistry. He also was a poet of amazing talent and ability. He returned to Sulaymaniyyah and began to teach.

After a few years he left all his studies behind and dedicated himself solely to the service of Allah. At the age of twenty-seven he decided to make the pilrimage to Mecca and to visit the Prophet (sas) in Medina. He met many Shaykhs and wise men on his travels and he always asked for their advice.

When he arrived in Medina he composed a poem in honor of the Prophet (sas) that impressed all who heard it and moved them to tears. He noticed one old man in particular and asked him for a piece of advice. This old man told him that it was time for him to travel on to Mecca. Once there, he must be careful not to be critical of any of the people he might see.

Shaykh Khalid (q) traveled on to the holy city of Mecca and performed the pilgimage. One day, as he was sitting near the Kaaba, reading the collection of praises of the Prophet (sas) called "Dalail al-Khayrat", he saw a man with a very black beard leaning against a pillar with his back to the Kaaba, staring at him. Shaykh Khalid (q) could not help but think to himself that the man was showing great disrespect to the House of God.

The man addressed him, scolding him for his critical thoughts. He said that the heart of the true believer is the real house of God and deserving of even more respect than the Kaaba. This is why the man faced towards Shaykh Khalid (q) instead. Shaykh Khalid (q) was astounded. The man knew his very thoughts. He knew the advice that had been given to him in Medina. Shaykh Khalid (q) rose and kissed the man's hands and feet. He asked to follow him and be his student. But the man answered that he was not Shaykh Khalid's (q) shaykh. Shaykh Khalid's (q) shaykh was still waiting for him, far away in India.

In 1224 AH/ 1809 CE, Shaykh Khalid left Mecca and began to travel overland towards India. He visited all the shaykhs, both living and dead, on his journey. He wrote many beautiful poems in praise of their refined characters and exalted stations.

In Delhi, Shaykh AbdAllah (q) felt the presence of a great soul approaching. He announced to his followers that the saint who would be his successor was coming. For over one year Shaykh Khalid (q) walked, over high mountains, down steep valleys, through dense forests and across barren deserts until he arrived at the Sultanate of Delhi. The night he finally arrived, he was so moved that he wrote a beautiful poem in praise of Shaykh AbdAllah (q), expressing his love and his yearning for Allah.

In five months of dedicated service to Shaykh AbdAllah (q), Shaykh Khalid (q) progressed through the stations of spiritual knowledge until he became one of the people of Divine Vision. Shaykh AbdAllah (q) sent him back to Iraq to be his representative, to guide the people to the Golden Chain and to the Naqshbandi Way.

For many years he lived and taught in the capital of Baghdad. Even the Sultan became his follower. Eventually he was drawn to Damascus because of its holiness. Many prophets, companions, and saints are buried there. His intention in moving was to die and be buried among them.

In the year 1242 AH / 1827 CE, a terrible disease began to sicken the people of Damascus. Many, many people became ill and most of them died. First Shaykh Khalid's (q) five-year-old son died, then his second son, followed by his wife and his daughter. The followers of the Shaykh begged him to ask Allah for safety for himself and his family, but he felt he could not because it had been his intention to die in Damascus.

One day soon afterwards, he announced to his family and followers that he had asked Allah to be allowed to collect all of the disease inside of his own body. He would die so that the rest of the people could live. He appointed Shaykh Ismail ash-Shirwani (q) as his successor and ordered them to follow him. He instructed them how and where to bury him when he died. They were to write above his grave only this one sentence, "This is the grave of Khalid, the stranger." Shaykh Khalid al-Baghdadi's (q) true home was in the Presence of Allah. He was a stranger and a traveler in this world.

He spent the night in the company of his close family. After the morning prayer he went into his room and ordered that no one should enter without his permission. He lay on his right side facing Mecca and prayed that all the sickness in the city come to him alone.

After two days of suffering, on the morning of Friday, he opened his eyes and said, "Allahu, Allahu, Allahu Haqq," the dhikr of the Shaykhs of the Golden Chain as they had been taught by Abu Bakr as-Siddiq (ra). Then his soul returned to its Lord, "well pleased and well pleasing" (89:27-30).

Shaykh Khalid (q) died on Friday, the 13th of Dhul-Qida, 1242 AH / 1827 CE. His funeral was attended by three hundred thousand (300,000) people. They buried him on a windy mountaintop overlooking the city of Damascus with the epitaph he had requested. After his death there were no more deaths in the city from that terrible sickness. In a great miracle, Allah had allowed Shaykh Khalid (q) to take upon himself all the sickness and to spare the people of Damascus.

Shaykh Khalid (q) passed the light and the secret of the Golden Chain to his successor, Shaykh Ismail ash-Shirwani (q).

May Allah bless, an-Nabi (sas), Siddiq (ra), Salman (ra), Qasim (ra), Jafar (ra), Tayfur (q), Abul Hasan (q), Abu Ali (q), Yusuf (q), Abul Abbas al-Khidr (as), Abdul Khaliq (q), Arif (q), Mahmoud (q), Ali (q), Muhammad Baba as-Samasi (q), Sayyid Amir Kulal (q), Shah Bahauddin an-Naqshband (q), Alauddin (q), Ya'qub (q), UbaydAllah (q), Muhammad az-Zahid (q), Darwish Muhammad (q), Muhammad al-Amkanaki (q), Muhammad al-Baqi (q), Ahmad al-Faruqi (q), Muhammad Ma'sum (q), Sayfuddin (q), Nur Muhammad (q), Habib Allah (q), AbdAllah (q), and Shaykh Khalid (q).

164 Links of Light: The Golden Chain

32
Ismail ash-Shirwani (q)

Shaykh Ismail (q) was born on a Tuesday, the seventh day of Dhul-Qida in the year 1201 AH / 1787 CE. He was born into a prominent family in the town of Kurdemir in the Khanate of Shirwan in the mountains of Caucasia. He was educated from an early age by his father, who was one of the greatest scholars of his day. He finished memorizing the Quran by the age of seven. At nine he was able to give rulings in legal desputes, quoting Quran and Hadith to support his judgement.

He grew into a tall man, muscular and strong. His skin was pale but his hair, beard and eyes were a glossy black. His voice was high and clear. He joined his father and began to teach in one of the universities in his area. Then one day everything changed. A state of attraction descended upon him and he became wrapped in a total absorbtion in Allah. Shaykh Ismail (q) lost all interest in the world around him; all he thought about, all he cared about, was Allah. He withdrew to quiet, isolated places to pray. He began to wander the mountains, looking always for the Reality that he could see clearly only in his own heart.

One day he had a vision in which he was told that his Shaykh was waiting for him in the city of Delhi in far-off India. This vision kept reappearing until, at the age of seventeen, Shaykh Ismail (q) finally got permission from his father to follow his vision. Shaykh Ismail (q) set off walking, carrying with him only a little money and food. Although he traveled day and night, it still took him a year to reach the city of Delhi.

In Delhi, Shaykh Ismail (q) found Shaykh AbdAllah ad-Dahlawi (q). He dedicated himself to his service. He lived in the guesthouse attached to his mosque. He served him and sat at his feet to learn spiritual wisdom. In 1224 AH/ 1809 CE, he was there when Shaykh Khalid al-Baghdadi (q) arrived at the home of Shaykh AbdAllah (q). Shaykh Ismail (q) watched his every move with fascination and respect. Shaykh Khalid (q) acted at all times with perfect manners and absolute sincerity. When Shaykh AbdAllah (q) ordered Shaykh Khalid (q) to return to Baghdad he also told Shaykh Ismail (q) to follow him.

Shaykh Ismail (q) set out from India, walking. In every place he stopped the light from his shining face attracted people. He would stay for a short while to teach them about the Shaykhs of the Golden Chain and to lead them to the Naqshbandi Way. In one village the people were desperate for rain. They had not seen a drop of moisture for a whole year. They asked Shaykh Ismail (q) to pray for them. As soon as he raised his hands the clouds began to form. It rained solidly for seven days.

When he reached Shirwan, his family was overjoyed at his return. He stayed with them for a few years until he felt the spiritual call of Shaykh Khalid (q), ordering him to come. He left his family again and set out on foot for Baghdad. In each village through which he passed he spent some time teaching them, inspiring them and renewing their faith. Finally after one year, he arrived in Baghdad. Shaykh Khalid (q) was expecting him and greeted him as his inheritor and successor. He took Shaykh Ismail (q) into his house and kept close company with him. After a few years they moved together to Damascus.

Shaykh Khalid (q) made Shaykh Ismail (q) his deputy, to teach and guide the seekers who came. Shaykh Ismail (q) said, "I am like a polished mirror. Whatever my master Khalid (q) has engraved upon me, that is what I, in turn, reflect to you." Shaykh Khalid (q) predicted that Shaykh Ismail (q) would renew the faith of Islam in all the territories of the Caucasus and guide them to the Naqshbandi Way. This would later serve as the foundation for their firm and steadfast opposition to the Russian invasions that would threaten them for the next century.

When Shaykh Khalid (q) passed away, Shyakh Ismail (q) could not keep from crying, but he pulled himself together in order to dispel the sadness and despair that threatened his followers. After staying some time in Damascus, Shaykh Ismail (q) returned to his homeland where, as his Shaykh had predicted, he was desperately needed.

Shaykh Ismail (q) established a mosque and a teaching center in the area of Shirwan. There people from all over came to sit with him and learn the spiritual sciences. He did not, however, always teach them in the way they expected. One day Shaykh Ismail (q) announced that he felt the need to test the strength of his reliance on God. In truth, he wanted to show his followers what it actually means to put your trust completely in God. He left his mosque and climbed high into the mountains above Shirwan. He continued climbing until he arrived at an isolated cave in which a family of lions had made their home. His students, following at a safe distence, hid quickly behind some rocks as they watched him lie down directly in front of the mouth of the cave.

The mother lion began to roar savagely as she drew her cubs protectively near her. The father lion nudged her to stop roaring. Together they sat and watched Shaykh Ismail (q) in eery silence. The students held their breaths in terror. The father lion approached the prone figure of the Shaykh and sniffed at him with interest. Then, to the astonishment of the hidden students, the father lion stretched himself out on the ground along side Shaykh Ismail (q). They lay together breathing in unison, the warm, heavy breathing of the lion and the soft, even breathing of the Shaykh. They lay like this for some time until Shaykh Ismail (q) got up quietly and returned to his mosque.

Another time, Shaykh Ismail (q) was passing through a village. The villagers ran after him begging him to stay and teach them. He answered them, "God has two ways of teaching; the common way which is the way you understand, and the uncommon, or special way, which is my way. Follow me if you can." The villagers quickly fell in behind him. After going a short distance, they came to a rushing river. Shaykh Ismail (q) stepped onto the water and, as if it was still the road, he walked across the river to the other side. He turned back and said, "This is the Way of God." The villagers stood on the bank and watched him disappear on the other side. That day they learned something about the nature of learning and the nature of Reality.

Shaykh Ismail (q) died on the tenth of the Dhul-Hijj, the day of Eid, 1255 AH / 1840 CE. He was buried in the town of Amasya. Before he died he said, " On the orders of the Prophet (sas), Abdul Khaliq al-Ghujdawani (q), Shah Naqshband (q), and my Shaykh, Khalid al-Baghdadi (q), in the spiritual presence of Uways al-Qarni (ra), I am passing the secret of the Golden Chain to three people at once. Although all of them will have the secret at the same time, they will only carry its authority one at a time. Shaykh Khas Muhammad (q) will follow me first, Shaykh Muhammad Effendi al-Yaraghi (q) will come second, and

Shaykh Sayyid Jamaluddin al-Ghumuqi (q) will come third."

This is just the way it happened. What amazed people most, was that he predicted precisely the order in which these men would eventually leave this world.

May Allah bless, an-Nabi (sas), Siddiq (ra), Salman (ra), Qasim (ra), Jafar (ra), Tayfur (q), Abul Hasan (q), Abu Ali (q), Yusuf (q), Abul Abbas al-Khidr (as), Abdul Khaliq (q), Arif (q), Mahmoud (q), Ali (q), Muhammad Baba as-Samasi (q), Sayyid Amir Kulal (q), Shah Bahauddin an-Naqshband (q), Alauddin (q), Ya'qub (q), UbaydAllah (q), Muhammad az-Zahid (q), Darwish Muhammad (q), Muhammad al-Amkanaki (q), Muhammad al-Baqi (q), Ahmad al-Faruqi (q), Muhammad Ma'sum (q), Sayfuddin (q), Nur Muhammad (q), Habib Allah (q), AbdAllah (q), Shaykh Khalid (q), and Shaykh Ismail (q).

170 Links of Light: The Golden Chain

33

Khas Muhammad ash-Shirwani (q)

Shaykh Khas Muhammad (q) was born in Kulal, in the district of Shirwan on Monday the first of Muharram, 1201 AH / 1786 CE. He grew into a tall and handsome young man. His beard was black but became streaked with white at an early age. His eyes were very dark and piercing. He attended the best schools and was trained in Islamic Law. His judgement was respected even at the young age of twenty.

He met Shaykh Ismail (q) when they were both young men. After that he remained constant in his practice of dhikr and remembrance. He spent all his free time in prayer and dhikr. He did not even stop to eat or rest. For twenty years, he ate only once a week. He made three hundred and fifty (350) rakats of prayer in every day. He used to say that the Way of the Golden Chain is not about complicated ideas or impressive words. It is not about repeating, "my shaykh said this," or "my shaykh said that." It is about being hungry and tired and giving up the easy ways of the world. It is about becoming totally reliant only on Allah, for everything.

He said that the Naqshbandi Way is based on four rules of behaviour: do not eat unless you are weak with hunger; do not sleep until you are overcome with tiredness; do not speak unless you are spoken to; but do not keep quiet when you are in the Presence of Allah, because you must ask from Him always, for all good things. A person cannot be called wise until there is not one thing, thought, or feeling left inside him that is displeasing to God.

A companion of the Shaykh was traveling on business from one city to another. His path took him through a deep, dark forest. It began to snow heavily and then the snow turned to rain. Between the melting snow and the pouring rain, the road became a river of rushing water. He kept riding until the road ended in a bridge over a small stream. With all the rain and flooding, the bridge had been washed away and the small stream had become a raging torrent. Afraid to go back into the dark forest to look for another crossing, he urged his horse into the river. The water quickly came up the legs of the horse and then up over the boots and legs of its rider. In his terrible fear he called out to Shaykh Khas Muhammad (q) to save him.

Suddenly he heard a voice behind him calling his name. He turned in the saddle and saw a huge figure of Shaykh Khas Muhammad (q). His fear began to get the better of him. Shaykh Khas Muhammad (q) reached out, took his hand and said sternly, "When you are with us you must feel no fear." Together the Shaykh, his companion, and the horse rose above the rushing waves. They walked swiftly over the top of the water until they reached the other side. Then the figure of Shaykh Khas Muhammad (q) disappeared.

The man continued on his journey until he reached the mosque of Shaykh Khas Muhammad (q). There he found the Shaykh sitting, warm and dry. He asked how he had been able to come so quickly to his rescue in that fearful forest. Shaykh Khas Muhammad (q) replied that he was not restricted by the normal boundaries of time and space. He could be anywhere he needed to be, at any time. Even though he lived in a remote area of the world he was not restricted by this physical reality. He could fulfill his duties as an inheritor of the cloak of the Prophet (sas), and watch over the souls in his care wherever they lived.

Shaykh Khas Muhammad (q) continued the work of Shaykh Ismail (q), spreading a deep love for, and understanding of, Islam in the Caucasus. Even in the remote villages people followed the teaching of the Shaykhs and the Way of the Prophet (sas). When the Russians invaded they found the people like a strong rock wall. Each one was obedient to his Shaykh, holding his place firmly, stone upon stone, without fear. They were ready to die to protect the freedom to pray and worship God as they believed right. Shaykh Khas Muhammad (q) was one of the great builders of this mighty wall of belief and brotherhood.

In 1259 AH /1843 CE, Shaykh Khas Muhammad (q) decided to make a pilgimage to Mecca and Medina. On his way home the following year he fell sick in the holy city of Damascus. On Sunday the third of Ramadan, in 1260 CE/ 1844 CE, Shaykh Khas Muhammad (q) returned to his Lord. He was buried in the blessed cemetery of Damascus, near many of the companions and family of the Prophet (sas). The secret of the Golden Chain and the authority to guide the believers passed to Shaykh Muhammad Effendi al-Yaraghi (q), just as Shaykh Ismail (q) had said it would.

May Allah bless, an-Nabi (sas), Siddiq (ra), Salman (ra), Qasim (ra), Jafar (ra), Tayfur (q), Abul Hasan (q), Abu Ali (q), Yusuf (q), Abul Abbas al-Khidr (as), Abdul Khaliq (q), Arif (q), Mahmoud (q), Ali (q), Muhammad Baba as-Samasi (q), Sayyid Amir Kulal (q), Shah Bahauddin an-Naqshband (q), Alauddin (q), Ya'qub (q), UbaydAllah (q), Muhammad az-Zahid (q), Darwish Muhammad (q), Muhammad al-Amkanaki (q), Muhammad al-Baqi (q), Ahmad al-Faruqi (q), Muhammad Ma'sum (q), Sayfuddin (q), Nur Muhammad (q), Habib Allah (q), AbdAllah (q), Shaykh Khalid (q), Shaykh Ismail (q), and Khas Muhammad (q).

34
Muhammad Effendi al-Yaraghi (q)

Shaykh Muhammad Effendi (q) was born in Kural in the district of Shirwan, on Tuesday, the second of Dhul Qida, in the year 1191 AH / 1777 CE. He studied Quran and Hadith. He also studied Chemistry, Astronomy, and Logic, until he was a master of all the sciences, spiritual and physical. He was a tall man with dark hair and dark beard, both of which turned snow white at an early age. His eyes were green and his voice was soft and kind.

He became a student of Shaykh Ismail ash-Shirwani (q) as a young man and served him with love and sincerity all of his life. Before he died, Shaykh Ismail (q) gave to Shaykh Muhammad Effendi (q) the secret and the light of the Golden Chain but not its authority. Shaykh Khas Muhammad (q) became the grand-shaykh and Shaykh Muhammad Effendi (q) served him faithfully until his death four years later.

In 1260 AH / 1844 CE Shaykh Muhammad Effendi (q) became the head of the Naqshbandi Sufi Order. He established a teaching center that, although located in this remote mountain nation, attracted people from all over the Muslim world. He rarely slept more than two hours a night. He ate little and sometimes only drank water. He wore a rough woolen robe in both summer and winter. He was humble towards everyone. In answer to his prayers, Allah healed the sick and restored sight to the blind.

The mountains of the Caucasus form a wall running between the Black and the

Caspian seas. A high craggy mountain range, it has steep, dangerous passes winding through it. The people live in fortified villages built in inaccessable places on the rocky peaks. They pasture their animals in the green river valleys far below in winter and the high mountain pastures in summer. In only a few places are there conditions that allow for gardens and orchards.

In the eighteenth and nineteenth centuries, the area served as a natural border between the three powerful empires of Persia, Ottoman Turkey, and Tsarist Russia. These three empires, two of them Muslim and the other Orthodox Christian, struggled with each other to control the mountainous border area. If they controlled the passes no one could get in or out without their permission.

After centuries of invasions from every side, the people of the Caucasus were used to conflict. All their men were trained from an early age to be skilled horsemen, archers and swordsmen. All their women were expected to be strong and independent, often able to stand beside their men and fight if they were needed.

Shaykh Muhammad Effendi (q) trained both men and women in the Islamic sciences and the practises of the Golden Chain. For months at a time, his most promising students would be secluded in small rooms, given little to eat and many prayers and beautiful dhikrs to perform. Because it was not the accepted custom to put women in seclusion, corrupt people began to imagine all kinds of improper things. The governor of Daghestan suspected that the men and women were really partying instead of praying. He sent his messenger to Shaykh Muhammad Effendi (q) ordering him to come and defend himself against these charges.

The Shaykh gave the messenger a sealed box that the governor was instructed not to open until the day of the trial. When the governor received the box he was very tempted to open it but a certain fear kept him from following his temptation. The day of the trial arrived. Shaykh Muhammad Effendi (q) entered the court and stood before the governor.

Shaykh Muhammad (q) told the governor it was time to open the box. Inside the governor found a letter. Under the letter he found a red-hot glowing coal. Under the coal was a piece of cloth and under that was a mound of gunpowder. The governor's hands began to shake and all the color drained from his face. For over a week he had been holding what was essentially a lighted bomb.

The letter said that if the Shaykh could keep fire from burning paper and cloth and from setting off the gunpowder, then he certainly could keep men and women from turning their eyes away from Allah. The governor and the court dismissed the charges against Shaykh Muhammad (q) without further argument.

In September 1830 CE Shaykh Muhammad Effendi (q) prayed the dawn prayer and lay back down to rest. He saw Shaykh Ismail (q) appear before him accompanied by the Prophet (sas) and Salman al-Farsi (ra). Salman (ra) reminded Shaykh Muhammad (q) of how he had helped protect the first Muslims by suggesting they dig a long ditch to keep the enemy from invading Madina. This battle, which came to be called the Battle of the Ditch, kept the Meccan army at bay until they were so demoralised that they went home without fighting. "You must do the same," he told Shaykh Muhammad (q). Shaykh Ismail (q) told him, on orders from the Prophet (sas), to lead his people against the Russian invaders as a religious duty. Their country would be the ditch that would keep the Muslim world safe from the expansion of Christian Russia.

Shaykh Muhammad (q) used to say to his followers, "Love is the light of the heart of a believer. A true Muslim is one who has surrendered his heart so totally to Allah that he cannot be the source of harm to anyone." Inspite of this he found himself in a country torn by war and violence. The Russian army had already taken hundreds of villages by force, burning them to the ground and killing or sending their citizens into exile. It was the explicit aim of the Tsar to get rid of any Muslim population on his borders. Shaykh Muhammad Effendi (q), this man of peace, after years of forbidding fighting and insisting on co-existence, was the one ordered by God to declare Jihad, or war, against the cruel invaders of his country.

At night Shaykh Muhammad Effendi (q) led his people in dhikr and prayer, teaching them to give up their individual wills to the Will of their Lord. During the day he counseled the brave mountaineers in the tactics of warfare. In this way he tried to turn the angry, vengeful, tribesmen into noble warriors, fighting in the way of the Prophet (sas), on the path of Allah, for the freedom and safety of their families and mercy for all creatures.

There is a story about Sayyidina Ali (ra), which exemplifies the nature of such a warrior. It was the custom of the early Arabs, before they engaged in battle, to send two champions to fight while the rest of the army looked on. At one battle, in the time of the Prophet (sas), Sayyidina Ali (ra) was the Muslim champion. He faced a young man from the enemy and together they fought with swords until Sayyidina Ali got the upper hand. As he was ready to deal the final blow his opponent spit in his face and insulted the Prophet (sas).

Sayyidina Ali (ra) felt the anger rise up inside of him. He put his sword back in its sheath. His enemy, lying on the ground waiting for the deathblow, was astonished. Sayyidina Ali (sas) said that if he killed his enemy in that state it would not be for Allah and justice but rather for revenge. He would not dishonor his Prophet (sas) by such an action.

His young enemy had never before seen such nobility and self-control. He rose to his feet and accepted Islam right there on the battlefield with all his astonished family watching. This was the way Shaykh Muhammad Effendi (q) taught the men of the Caucasus; to only fight in order to defend themselves and their families, without anger and without fear.

Shaykh Muhammad Effendi al-Yaraghi (q) died on the 17th of Muharram 1265 AH / 1848 CE. Just as Shaykh Ismail (q) had predicted, the authority of the Golden Chain passed to his deputy, Shaykh Jamaluddin al-Ghumuqi (q).

May Allah bless, an-Nabi (sas), Siddiq (ra), Salman (ra), Qasim (ra), Jafar (ra), Tayfur (q), Abul Hasan (q), Abu Ali (q), Yusuf (q), Abul Abbas al-Khidr (as), Abdul Khaliq (q), Arif (q), Mahmoud (q), Ali (q), Muhammad Baba as-Samasi (q), Sayyid Amir Kulal (q), Shah Bahauddin an-Naqshband (q), Alauddin (q), Ya'qub (q), UbaydAllah (q), Muhammad az-Zahid (q), Darwish Muhammad (q), Muhammad al-Amkanaki (q), Muhammad al-Baqi (q), Ahmad al-Faruqi (q), Muhammad Ma'sum (q), Sayfuddin (q), Nur Muhammad (q), Habib Allah (q), AbdAllah (q), Shaykh Khalid (q), Shaykh Ismail (q), Khas Muhammad (q), and Shaykh Muhammad Effendi al-Yaraghi (q).

180 Links of Light: The Golden Chain

35
Jamaluddin al-Ghumuqi al-Husayni (q)

Shaykh Jamaluddin (q) was born in the town of Gazikumuk in Daghestan in 1203 AH / 1788 CE, on Thursday the 16th of Muharram. When he was a baby it was clear that he was unlike other children. Allah had given him two extra eyes, one above his bellybutton and one just below. The one above could see into the heavenly worlds and the one below could see all things in the worlds of men and jinn. Women came from all over his area to have a peak at this remarkable baby. When he was older he could answer questions about anything that had happened in the past or would happen in the future, in this world and the next, just by looking with these special eyes.

Shaykh Jamaluddin (q) had an even more precious gift; he could see with the eyes of his heart. Unlike most babies who are born with knowledge of where they came from but are veiled little by little by the diversions of the world, Shaykh Jamaluddin was never veiled. He remembered clearly his heavenly origins and the One Who made us all. He continued all his life, to see the Divine Reality with the eyes of his heart.

Shaykh Jamaluddin (q) was descended from the Prophet (sas) through his grandson Husayn (as). He was very learned and could speak fifteen languages. He was a doctor and mathematician as well as a scholar of Quran and Hadith. He also had a very impressive appearance, very tall and very thin, with a long, wide beard. The color of his eyes, if you were able to look into them, was red. His voice was soft and sweet.

For a while, as a young man, he worked as a secretary to the governor of his province. However, because of his ability to see the Truth he could not stand to work for him for very long. He told the governor what he thought about politics and politicians and then he resigned. The governor was greatly offended and never forgot or forgave Shaykh Jamaluddin (q). He continued to make life difficult for the Shaykh throughout his long life.

Shaykh Jamaluddin (q) found Shaykh Ismail (q) and attached himself to his service. He was his deputy for many years until he reached high stations of knowledge and vision. Before he died, Shaykh Ismail (q) gave him both the secret and the light of the Golden Chain. He became the deputy in turn, of Shaykh Khas Muhammad (q) and then of Shaykh Muhammad Effendi (q). He aided them both in teaching the people and leading them to the path of righteous war, Jihad, against the invading Russians.

One day he was sitting with his students in a garden. They were eating from a bowl of apples. Suddenly Shaykh Jamaluddin (q) took two apples. He threw one high into the air and far away. His companions were shocked. To throw food is a wasteful action, and worse, disrespectful to Allah who took the care to create it and generously provide it for them to eat. After a short while, Shaykh Jamaluddin (q) took the other apple and repeated his strange action. His companions began to grumble among themselves. He warned them to be careful not to judge what they did not understand.

After a few hours a man came running into the garden, crying. His brother had died two hours before and he wanted the Shaykh to pray for his soul. Then Shaykh Jamaluddin (q) revealed the secret behind his earlier actions. He had seen Azrail (as), the angel of death, coming to take the soul of the brother with anger and punishment. Shaykh Jamaluddin (q) threw the apple to attract the attention of the angel and stop him. He asked that he return to his Lord and say that Shaykh Jamaluddin (q) wanted to change the nature of the brother's death. Azrail (as) did as the Shaykh asked and he returned to take the soul of the brother, this time, with mercy and gentleness. Shaykh Jamaluddin (q) threw the second apple to stop the angel again. This time the Shaykh asked to be permitted to take the soul of the brother with his own hand. In this way the brother died without the terror of seeing the fearsome form of the angel of death. He died in a state of joy, easily accepting death at the hands of his beloved

Shaykh.

Shaykh Jamaluddin (q) did not have much time, however, to enjoy the peaceful gardens of his native land. The war against the invading Russians was escalating. Since the death of Shaykh Ismail (q) all three of his saintly deputies had worked hard educating and preparing their people to obey God's Will and fight as righteous warriors. War is not something that any sane person desires. The Shaykhs always counsel peace and compromise, following the example of the Prophet Muhammmad (sas). When, however, those possibilities are exhausted then the Shaykhs, like the Prophet (sas) before them, have no alternative but to support the Truth with force. Whatever Allah gives, the Saints humbly accept, be it war or peace, poverty or plenty, life or death. In all circumstances the goal is to obey the Divine Law and follow the perfect example of the Prophet (sas).

Jihad is a word that is used often these days but rarely understood. The word itself means to struggle, to tire yourself out in an effort to accomplish something. To tire yourself out talking and persuading, working and praying, is the first requirement. When those fail, only then, can physical defense be considered. To be called a Jihad in God's name the purpose must be legally, as well as morally, sound. The first requirement for a righteous Jihad must be a righteous government, one that speaks for all of the people and one that is dedicated to following the Islamic Way. Secondly, the nation must be under military attack by an enemy whose express wish is to suppress the practice of Islam and to expel the Muslims from their homes.

One of Shaykh Jamaluddin's (q) students was named Shamil. He had spent many years with the Shaykh, studying Quran and Hadith and learning self-discipline and obedience to God's Will. He was chosen to lead the warriors of the Caucasus in their fight for religious freedom. His appointment was the last piece needed to fulfill the laws that determine Jihad. He was a righteous leader, who could speak for his countrymen and expect to be obeyed.

For forty years the brave men and women of the Caucasus obeyed their leader Shamil and obeyed their Shaykhs. They defended their country against a Russian army that was much larger and much better armed. When they hid in the dense forests in order to ambush the larger army, the Russians began to chop down the trees. When they retreated to their mountain fortresses, they were beseiged with cannon and modern weapons. The Russian government spared no cost in their effort to destroy the small nation in the Caucasus, tree by tree, stone by stone, man by man.

Shaykh Jamaluddin (q) assured Shamil that as long as the people remained unified and did their prayers and their dhikr they could not be defeated. But little by little the long war wore down the resolve of the people. They were tired of hardship, of war and sacrifice. One by one the villages began to surrender to the enemy, until Shamil was left with a small army holed up in an isolated mountain fort, desperately defending their wives and children. Rather than see all the innocent families killed, Shamil gave himself up to be executed, he thought, in exchange for their freedom. But just like the enemy warrior who had fought Sayyidina Ali (ra) so long before, Shamil's Russian foe had come to admire his bravery, his nobility and his principles. They did not kill him, his followers, or their families. Rather he was escorted like a hero across Russia into the presence of the Tsar. He was kept under a comfortable house arrest until released to exile in Arabia. He died in Madina many years later and was buried among the family and companions of the Prophet (sas) in the cemetary of Baqi.

Shaykh Jamaluddin (q) also left the Caucasus, to settle with his family in the city of Istanbul in Turkey. On the fifth of Shawwal, 1285 AH / 1869 CE, at the age of eighty, Shaykh Jamaluddin called his wife and daughter to his side. He told them that the previous night a large passenger ship had foundered in the Bosphorous. He had labored all night bringing its many passengers to the safety of the shore. His energy was exhausted and it was his time to leave this life.

The day after his death, his family read in the newspapers about the sinking of the great ship and how an unknown man had been responsible for saving the lives of the passengers. Miraculously not one person had drowned. Only his family knew that the brave and selfless stranger who had given his life for the lives of the shipwrecked people was Shaykh Jamaluddin (q). It was not surprising that this great saint, who had spent most of his life surrounded by war, readily gave his life to save others.

Shaykh Jamaluddin (q) passed the light and the secret of the Golden Chain to his deputy, Shaykh Ahmad as-Sughuri (q).

May Allah bless, an-Nabi (sas), Siddiq (ra), Salman (ra), Qasim (ra), Jafar (ra), Tayfur (q), Abul Hasan (q), Abu Ali (q), Yusuf (q), Abul Abbas al-Khidr (as), Abdul Khaliq (q), Arif (q), Mahmoud (q), Ali (q), Muhammad Baba as-Samasi (q), Sayyid Amir Kulal (q), Shah Bahauddin an-Naqshband (q), Alauddin (q), Ya'qub (q), UbaydAllah (q), Muhammad az-Zahid (q), Darwish Muhammad (q), Muhammad al-Amkanaki (q), Muhammad al-Baqi (q), Ahmad al-Faruqi (q), Muhammad Ma'sum (q), Sayfuddin (q), Nur Muhammad (q), Habib Allah (q), AbdAllah (q), Shaykh Khalid (q), Shaykh Ismail (q), Khas Muhammad (q), Shaykh Muhammad Effendi al-Yaraghi (q), and Shaykh Jamaluddin al-Ghumuqi al-Husayni (q).

36

Abu Ahmad as-Sughuri (q)

Shaykh Abu Ahmad (q) was born in Sughur, a town in Daghestan, on Wednesday, the 3rd of Rajab, in 1207 AH / 1793 CE. When he was young he could often see the sacred Name of Allah written in light between heaven and earth. This great reminder made him very humble. By the age of thirty he had attained the state of annihilation, or complete disappearance in God. When anyone tried to take his photograph no picture would appear. When anyone tried to even draw his likeness either the pencil would not write or the sketch would vanish from the paper by the next morning.

He attached himself spiritually to Shaykh Jamaluddin (q) and never let go. When Shaykh Jamaluddin (q) had to escape the Caucasus and flee to Turkey, Shaykh Abu Ahmad (q) stayed behind as his representative. He helped his people deal with the hardships that Russian occupation caused and he made sure that their faith and hope remained strong.

He educated thousands of people in Islam and the way of the Golden Chain. He was both their spiritual guide and a great warrior who defended them against the Russian oppression. His real joy, however, was to spend time alone with his Lord, in peaceful meditation and worship. Because of his political involvement the Russians often had him put under house arrest. In fact nothing could have pleased him more.

The people of his area loved him greatly. Everytime the Russians took him prisoner, his people mourned. Everytime he was released, they rejoiced. No matter how closely he was guarded, no matter how many restrictions were placed upon him, visitors always found him well supplied with warm clothing and ample food. In explanation of this mystery he would say that God provides for those who struggle in His Way.

One time the Russians arrested him. They put him in a carriage in order to take him away. His people stood on every side crying as if their hearts were being torn from their bodies. Shaykh Abu Ahmad (q) kept searching the crowd with his eyes, looking for someone who had not arrived. The driver urged the horses forward. They did not move. He shouted at them. They stood still. The driver resorted to whipping the horses to make them obey. They remained unmoving. Whatever the driver did the horses would not respond. Shaykh Abu Ahmad (q) told the driver to stop punishing the horses. They were under the Shaykh's command and they would do nothing until he released them.

After several hours a young soldier arrived. Shaykh Abu Ahmad (q) called him over and scolded him. He was the son of a follower of Shaykh Abu Ahmad (q) and yet he had enlisted in the Russian army. He was helping to oppress his own people. Shaykh Abu Ahmad (q) told him that he was destined to be a saint. He must leave the army and change his life around. The young man tore off his uniform and took the Shaykh's hand promising to listen and obey. Shaykh Abu Ahmad replied calmly that of course he would, even the horses listened and obeyed. The wild animals of the forest even listened and obeyed because every word that he uttered was in direct obedience to God. The young man was arrested and put into the carriage with the Shaykh. Only then did Shaykh Abu Ahmad (q) allow the horses to obey the driver. Quickly the carriage sped out of town.

During this period of time the area of the Caucasus came to be called the Birthplace of Saints because so many saints lived there. Shaykhs, Ismail (q), Khas Muhammad (q), Muhammad Effendi (q), Jamaluddin (q) and Abu Ahmad (q) were all born within six years of each other in this small corner of the world. Together they led the Naqshbandi Order, protecting and blessing the whole world from their isolated mountain home, while they guided their own people in that rare instance when spiritual and physical struggle combine for a brief moment of supreme nobility and honor, Jihad.

Shaykh Abu Ahmad (q) died in Sughur on the 17th of Rabi al-Awwal, 1299 AH / 1882 CE, at the age of 92. He was buried in the town of his birth where his family continued to live. After many years his daughter had a dream in which she saw her father complaining that his gravestone had fallen over and was causing him pain. The next morning she went out to the graveyard and saw that indeed his grave had collapsed and his headstone had fallen over. To repair the grave they had to dig it up. They found the body of Shaykh Abu Ahmad (q) as fresh and clean as if he had only just been put in the ground that very day.

Before he died Shaykh Abu Ahmad (q) had appointed two of his deputies to inherit the light and the secret of the Golden Chain from him. The first to follow him would be Shaykh Abu Muhammad al-Madani (q). The second would be Shaykh Sharafuddin ad-Daghestani (q).

May Allah bless, an-Nabi (sas), Siddiq (ra), Salman (ra), Qasim (ra), Jafar (ra), Tayfur (q), Abul Hasan (q), Abu Ali (q), Yusuf (q), Abul Abbas al-Khidr (as), Abdul Khaliq (q), Arif (q), Mahmoud (q), Ali (q), Muhammad Baba as-Samasi (q), Sayyid Amir Kulal (q), Shah Bahauddin an-Naqshband (q), Alauddin (q), Ya'qub (q), UbaydAllah (q), Muhammad az-Zahid (q), Darwish Muhammad (q), Muhammad al-Amkanaki (q), Muhammad al-Baqi (q), Ahmad al-Faruqi (q), Muhammad Ma'sum (q), Sayfuddin (q), Nur Muhammad (q), Habib Allah (q), AbdAllah (q), Shaykh Khalid (q), Shaykh Ismail (q), Khas Muhammad (q), Shaykh Muhammad Effendi al-Yaraghi (q), Sayyid Jamaluddin al-Ghumuqi al-Husayni (q), and Abu Ahmad as-Sughuri (q).

37

Abu Muhammad al-Madani (q)

Shaykh Abu Muhammad (q) was born in Kikunu, in Daghestan, in the year 1251 AH/ 1835 CE. Before his birth Shaykh Abu Ahmad (q), passing through Kikunu, predicted that a child would be born there who would be a great saint.

Not only did Shaykh Abu Muhammad (q) grow to resemble the Prophet (sas) in his spiritual presence but he also resembled the Prophet (sas) in his physical appearance as well. He was well built and very handsome, with dark almond eyes and a glowing smile, just as the beloved Prophet (sas) is described in the literature. He was strong and courageous. He fought against the invaders of his homeland with both his prayers and his actions.

When he was a young man two of his friends invited him to accompany them to visit Shaykh Abu Ahmad (q). When they arrived at his mosque the Shaykh greeted them and then called Abu Muhammad (q) to his side. He gave him initiation into the Naqshbandi Order right away and planted dhikr on his tongue. He gave nothing to his two friends. The Shaykh told them instead that they could receive all they needed from their companion Abu Muhammad (q). This caused his friends to feel quite jealous.

The three friends went their separate ways. Some years later when no rain had fallen for a long time in their village, the two jealous friends decided to test Abu Muhammad (q), to see if he really was a shaykh. They set out on the road to his house. On the way they passed by a village in which they caught a glimpse through an open window of a beautiful girl getting dressed. They stopped and, hiding in the bushes, they watched her in secret. Then they continued on their way.

They arrived at the house of Abu Muhammad (q) and knocked at the door. He answered by asking who was there? They looked at each other and snorted. How could he be a shaykh and not even know who was at his own door? They knocked again. This time Shaykh Abu Muhammad (q) called out their names, for certainly he knew them and their purpose. Then he told them that it is possible to be a shaykh and not know who is behind a door but it is not possible to be a shaykh and still peak in secret at a half naked woman.

The two friends were terribly ashamed. They could not even say anything about the drought in their village. They just turned around and headed for home. Shaykh Abu Muhammad (q) ran after them and promised to give them what they had came for. As soon as they reached their village, the clouds gathered and it began to rain.

Shaykh Abu Muhammad (q) grew up during the Jihad against the Russians. He was a brave warrior in those struggles. Even the Russians admired his bravery and were witness to some of his miracles. Many times they tried to kill him. Many times they arrested him. Finally they captured him and sent him far away, north to the icy wasteland of Siberia.

In this desolate place they still tried to keep him behind bars. No matter what they did they would find him outside, doing what he could to help the other prisoners and praying with them. They tried chaining him to the prison wall but still they found him walking outside deep in conversation with a stranger. Later he said that the stranger was actually Sayyidina Khidr (as) who would often come to keep him company. No matter what they tried they could not contain him. Finally, in frustration, they let him go free.

He returned briefly to visit his family and then set off for Turkey. He found a ship waiting for him at the Black Sea port. Its engine had refused to start until Shaykh Abu Muhammad (q) set foot on its deck. Then the ship not only began to work but it almost flew. The captain had a dream in which he saw the engine take the human shape of the Shaykh and actually sprout wings. They arrived in one day instead of the usual three.

Shaykh Abu Muhammad (q) stayed one year in the house of a kind friend before he journeyed on. Every morning during this time the friend would find two gold coins under his pillow. This man's family still has some of these miraculous coins to this day.

Finally he traveled on to Istanbul. The Ottoman Sultan, Abdul Hamid II, met him and was so impressed that he took his hand and was given initiation into the Naqshbandi Order. He offered Shaykh Abu Muhammad (q) any piece of land he wanted in order to build his home and his mosque. Shaykh Abu Muhammad (q) chose to live in an area between the cities of Yalowa and Bursa. There was no water in this place so Sayyidina Khidr (as) stabbed his walking stick into the earth and a spring gushed out. It is still running to this day.

They began building. The many families who had fled the Russian oppression in the Caucasus, now gathered around the mosque of Shaykh Abu Muhammad (q). After a while, there were 750 homes, two mosques and a school. He named the new village Rashadiya, (meaning rightly guided).

Every living thing in that village recited dhikr from the day it was born until the day it died. There was peace and harmony among the people. Even the dogs and cats did not fight. Every action performed was accompanied by dhikr, praising and remembering God. Mothers nursed their children with dhikr, baked their bread and mopped their floors with dhikr. Men tilled their fields and chopped wood with dhikr. Spiritual light streamed from this happy place.

One night during Ramadan Shaykh Abu Muhammad (q) was breaking fast at the house of a friend. He remarked that he could feel the whole village and all its surroundings joining him in praising their Lord, even the insects, even the plants, even the stones. He could feel, however, that there was one creature somewhere in the house that was so sad and depressed it could not join in the dhikr. If this creature was unhappy then Allah also was unhappy.

Shaykh Abu Muhammad (q) sent the owner of the house to look for this creature. In his young son's room he found a small box, inside of which he found a worm. This worm longed for its family and its safe home in the ground. The sadness of this one little worm was enough to disrupt the dhikr of the whole village. The Shaykh set the worm free, and in this way demonstrated that the welfare of all creatures is important to God, and consequently to people. The Shaykh is responsible for all of us. Any harm to any one, however tiny, causes harm to everyone.

Shaykh Abu Muhammad (q) died in 1331 AH / 1913 CE and was buried in Rashadiya. He passed the secret and the light of the Golden Chain to his nephew, Shaykh Sharafuddin (q).

May Allah bless, an-Nabi (sas), Siddiq (ra), Salman (ra), Qasim (ra), Jafar (ra), Tayfur (q), Abul Hasan (q), Abu Ali (q), Yusuf (q), Abul Abbas al-Khidr (as), Abdul Khaliq (q), Arif (q), Mahmoud (q), Ali (q), Muhammad Baba as-Samasi (q), Sayyid Amir Kulal (q), Shah Bahauddin an-Naqshband (q), Alauddin (q), Ya'qub (q), UbaydAllah (q), Muhammad az-Zahid (q), Darwish Muhammad (q), Muhammad al-Amkanaki (q), Muhammad al-Baqi (q), Ahmad al-Faruqi (q), Muhammad Ma'sum (q), Sayfuddin (q), Nur Muhammad (q), Habib Allah (q), AbdAllah (q), Shaykh Khalid (q), Shaykh Ismail (q), Khas Muhammad (q), Shaykh Muhammad Effendi al-Yaraghi (q), Sayyid Jamaluddin al-Ghumuqi al-Husayni (q), Abu Ahmad as-Sughuri (q), and Abu Muhammad al-Madani (q).

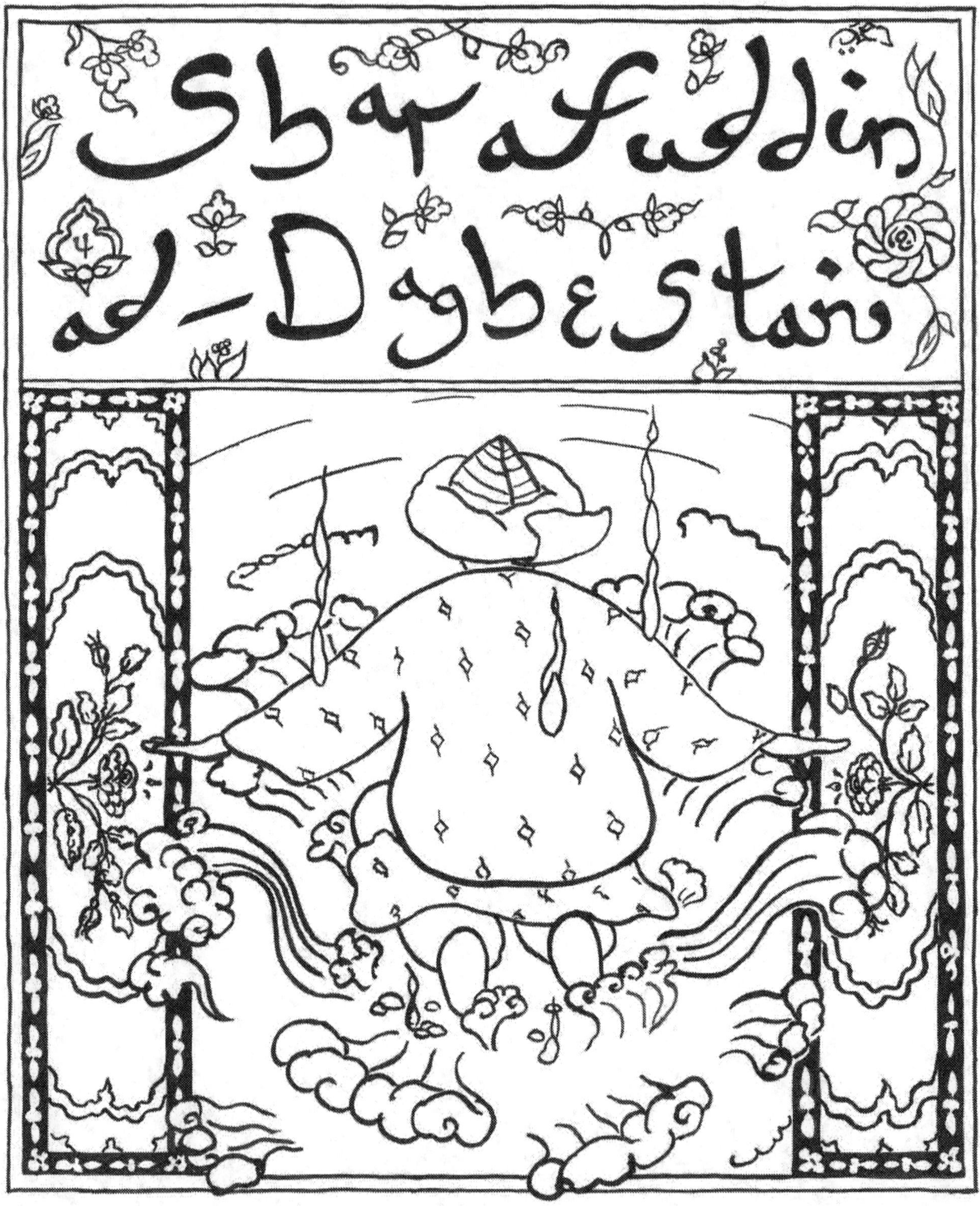
Sharafuddin
ad-Dagbestani
4

38

Sharafuddin ad-Daghestani (q)

Shaykh Sharafuddin (q) was born in Kikunu, Daghestan, on the third of Dhul Qida in the year 1292 AH /1875 CE. Shaykh Abu Muhammad al-Madani (q) was his uncle. As a baby he was heard to make shahada constantly, saying over and over, with the index finger of his right hand raised, *la ilaha illa Allah*. While he nursed he said only, Allah, Allah.

On one side he was the nephew of Shaykh Abu Muhammad (q). On the other side he was a descendant of Miqdad ibn al-Aswad (ra), a companion of the Prophet Muhammad (sas). Whenever the Prophet (sas) had to leave Madina he would put Miqdad (ra) in charge. One time he placed his blessed hand on Miqdad's (ra) shoulder and asked God's blessings for him and his descendants. After this, the imprint of the Prophet's (sas) hand would appear as a birthmark on the shoulders of certain of his descendants. Shaykh Sharafuddin (q) carried this mark and from it streamed a radiant light.

As he grew up he did not become veiled by the distractions of the world. He could hear the animals and the birds, the grass and the stones, even the mighty mountains themselves, making their own dhikrs, each one praising its Creator in its own unique way. The family of Shaykh Sharafuddin (q) lived in the mountains and it was necessary to store large quantities of wood to burn during the winter months to keep the family warm. It was the job of the children to collect much of this wood from the dense forests. His mother would send Shaykh Sharafuddin (q) but he would only bring her the old rotting branches he found lying on the ground. When his mother complained, he asked her how she could expect him to chop off the limbs of trees that he could clearly hear reciting dhikr Allah?

As he grew into manhood he was taught by the spiritual presences of both Shaykh Jamaluddin (q) and Shaykh Abu Ahmad (q). Under their close guidance he reached a state of pure love for God. He said that it felt as if his whole body was on fire with love. Sometimes it got too much for him and he would run to the river and jump into its icy waters in order to cool off. People nearby could hear a loud hiss of steam just as though a hot frying pan had been plunged into cold water.

His family finally decided to flee Daghestan and seek refuge in Turkey. To do this they had to travel by foot for five months, hiding during the daylight hours and moving only in the dark of night. They made it safely and joined Shaykh Abu Muhammad (q) in Rashadiya.

In Turkey Shaykh Sharafuddin (q) studied Quran and Hadith until he became universally recognized as a religious scholar. Sultan Abdul Hamid appointed him Shaykh al-Islam, the highest religious authority in the Ottoman Empire.

His uncle Shaykh Abu Muhammad (q) put him into seclusion many times in the mountains near Rashadiya. He reached spiritual heights that no one else had explored. He could see into the unknown to find things that were lost. He could see into the future to predict things that had yet to happen. He predicted that one of his spiritual descendants would carry Islam and the Naqshbandi Way to the West and from there to every corner of the globe.

During one seclusion that lasted six months, he experienced a vision of a poisonous snake, coiled and ready to strike, on his prayer carpet. He counseled himself saying, "There is no one to fear except Allah alone." Then he continued with his prayer, putting his face in sajda directly on the head of the hissing snake. Immediately the snake disappeared and all the heavens were opened to him. When he returned to Rashadiya after this seclusion his own shaykh, Shaykh Abu Muhammad (q), sat at his feet and became his follower. When he died Shaykh Abu Muhammad (q) left Shaykh Sharafuddin (q) in charge of the Naqshbandi Order and the peaceful town of Rashadiya.

Shaykh Sharafuddin (q) was light skinned with blue eyes and a black beard. As he grew older his beard turned completely white like soft cotton. At certain times his spiritual state was so exalted that no one could look into his eyes without losing their senses. When he was in these states he would cover his face with a cloth in order to protect his companions.

The mighty Ottoman Empire fell to a rebellion led by a man who called himself Ataturk. His goal was to modernise Turkey on the model of the European countries. In order to do this Ataturk made any outward show of religion against the law. No one in all of Turkey was allowed to even wear the head covering of the Prophet (sas), the turban. The only exception was Shaykh Sharafuddin (q). Even Ataturk could not help but show him respect. In spite of this Shaykh Sharafuddin (q) spent his last months in a Turkish jail.

Three months after he was released he told his nephew Shaykh AbdAllah (q) that he was dying. During his time in prison he had studied the secrets of the chapter of the Quran called *al-Anam*, the Cattle. From the oceans of knowledge that it contains he had been able to extract the names of all of the 7,007 Naqshbandi saints (qhm) who will appear in the last days with Sayyidina Mahdi (as). This effort had weakened him. Now he was passing the information to Shaykh AbdAllah (q) and advising him to leave Turkey for the Middle East as soon as an opportunity appeared.

On the 27th of Jumada al-Awwal 1355 AH/ 1936 CE, Shaykh Sharafuddin (q) died. His funeral prayer was attended by thousands. Even the government of Ataturk sent a delegation. He was buried in his beloved town of Rashadiya. He passed the secret and the light of the Golden Chain to his nephew, Shaykh AbdAllah al-Faiz ad-Daghestani (q).

May Allah bless, an-Nabi (sas), Siddiq (ra), Salman (ra), Qasim (ra), Jafar (ra), Tayfur (q), Abul Hasan (q), Abu Ali (q), Yusuf (q), Abul Abbas al-Khidr (as), Abdul Khaliq (q), Arif (q), Mahmoud (q), Ali (q), Muhammad Baba as-Samasi (q), Sayyid Amir Kulal (q), Shah Bahauddin an-Naqshband (q), Alauddin (q), Ya'qub (q), UbaydAllah (q), Muhammad az-Zahid (q), Darwish Muhammad (q), Muhammad al-Amkanaki (q), Muhammad al-Baqi (q), Ahmad al-Faruqi (q), Muhammad Ma'sum (q), Sayfuddin (q), Nur Muhammad (q), Habib Allah (q), AbdAllah (q), Shaykh Khalid (q), Shaykh Ismail (q), Khas Muhammad (q), Shaykh Muhammad Effendi al-Yaraghi (q), Sayyid Jamaluddin al-Ghumuqi al-Husayni (q),

Abu Ahmad as-Sughuri (q), Abu Muhammad al-Madani (q), and Shaykh Sharafuddin ad-Daghestani (q).

202 Links of Light: The Golden Chain

39
Abdallah al-Faiz ad-Daghestani (q)

Shaykh AbdAllah (q) was born to a prominent family in the small country of Daghestan in the year 1309 AH / 1891 CE. The men in his father's family were doctors and surgeons. In his mother's family they were saints and scholars. His mother's brother was Shaykh Sharafuddin (q). Shaykh Sharafuddin (q) told his sister that when she became pregnant she must be very careful of all she would say and do. The soul she would carry would be very special. Later when she did become pregnant her baby was born able to see clearly the heavenly worlds from which he had come. He continued to have this unique ability for the rest of his life. They named him AbdAllah, servant of God, and he had the mark of the Prophet's (sas) hand on his back, just as his uncle had.

Shaykh AbdAllah (q), even as a young child, was never heard to cry or complain. From the day he was born he did dhikr, constantly saying Allah, Allah. At seven months he was already speaking in complete sentences that everyone could understand. At three years he was giving advice to strangers that showed knowledge of the future. He knew people's names before they were introduced. He would always sit next to his uncle and take part in his spiritual discussions. By the age of seven he had already learned most of the Quran and the Law just by listening to what was going on around him.

People began to consult him to see if the action they were planning would have a successful outcome. He would be able to look and tell them if their marriages or business plans were written on the Preserved Tablets in heaven, if they were God's Will. His special gift, however, was that he was able to heal the sick. People found themselves cured, no matter how far away they lived, just by having him recite one *Fatihah* in their name.

One day his uncle requested that Shaykh AbdAllah (q) ask Allah if the time had come for them to leave their homeland to find refuge in Turkey. The Russian occupation had become so oppressive that all the spiritual light, that had radiated so profusely from that area just a few years before, was starting to be withdrawn. The Shaykhs were leaving the Caucasus. Although he was just a young child, Shaykh AbdAllah (q) prayed two rakats after the night prayer and asked Almighty God for guidance for himself and his people.

During that night he saw a vision in which the Prophet (sas) came to him and took him on a journey. Shaykh AbdAllah (q) was only four years old. He had never left his mountain home. He had never seen an ocean or the sea. To him what he was shown looked like a city of lights floating on an enormous river. Later he realized it was a boat on the sea. On this boat he recognised all the people of his village but there were many, many more people that he did not recognize. In the sky above the boat he saw what looked to him like a huge pumpkin made out of light. He cut pieces from the pumpkin and gave each person in the city a taste. All the people began to glow inwardly with its light. He was told that these were all the people of Daghestan and their children who were yet to be born, and their children's children. They were given permission to cross the Black Sea to a new life in Turkey. Also on this city of light, were all the people from all over the world who would now be able to find Shaykh AbdAllah (q) and take guidance and wisdom from him.

After this he was taken into the heavens on a Night Journey that mirrored the *Mihraj* of the Prophet (q). He was given all kinds of insights and wisdom. He saw this knowledge enter his heart in the form of words of light. These words first appeared to him to be glowing with a green light and then they gradually changed to a radiant purple. He entered into these words of light at the same time as they entered into him.

After this experience he did not need to read or study from books. The many meanings of Quran and Hadith, the intricacies of the sacred Law, all were revealed directly to his heart and mind without need for study or books. In this way he was given the station of the Prophet (sas) who was called *ummi*, meaning "unable to read." He did not need to read or write because the essential meaning of all words entered directly into his heart without the need for a vehicle such as pen or paper.

At the morning prayer he announced that the Prophet (sas) had given them permission to emigrate. Even though he was such a young child everyone in the village, without questioning, went home immediately and began preparing to travel. The trip to Turkey was dangerous and long. The Russian army patrolled the borders and shot at anything that moved. Robbers were also hiding in order to ambush and steal from these helpless refugees. By reciting a verse from *Surat Yasin* Shaykh Sharafuddin (q) kept the villagers hidden. They crossed safely into Turkey and settled near Shaykh Abu Muhammad (q) in Rashadiya.

At fifteen Shaykh AbdAllah (q) married. Six months later Shaykh Sharafuddin sent him into seclusion for five years. Without hesitation he left his sad mother and sobbing wife to obey the orders of his shaykh. He was sent to a cave high in the mountains above Rashadiya. He was ordered to take a shower six times a day with the icy cold water from melting snow and mountain streams. In additon to his usual prayers and dhikr he was told to read at least seven sections of the Quran, recite the name of Allah 148,000 times, and praise the Prophet (sas) 24,000 times each day. He was given seven olives and a slice of bread daily as his only food and he was not allowed to talk to anyone. He continued to live like this until he was twenty.

Many wonderous experiences were given to him in this seclusion. He had one vision in which he saw the Prophet (sas) as a young man. He would leave the city of Mecca and retreat alone to the cave on Mount Hira to pray. For forty days Shaykh AbdAllah (q) had the real experience of praying every prayer behind the Prophet (sas) in that cave. After five years Shaykh Abdallah (q) returned to his joyful wife and mother, but it was just the first in a very long life filled with spiritual seclusions.

Before he died, Shaykh Sharafuddin (q) told Shaykh AbdAllah (q) that he must leave Turkey as soon as he found an opening. He would be the one to bring the Golden Chain back to Arab lands. By the marriage of his daughter Shaykh AbdAllah (q) got permission to travel to Egypt and then on to Syria. The Prophet (sas) and Abu Bakr (ra), in a vision, showed him where to build his house, on the mountain of Qasyun above the city of Damascus. In this humble place, kings and princes, scholars from Europe and Asia, seekers from around the globe, all gathered to find the blessings and guidance of this remarkable saint.

There is a special dhikr, called the King of Dhikrs, which only the greatest of saints can accomplish. It is not at all like the kind of dhikr we do. With it the saints are able to recite the whole of the Quran, with all of its secrets and inner realities. Each of the 600,000 letters of the Quran carries within it 12,000 secrets. To do this dhikr properly each of these secrets must appear within the heart as its letter is being pronounced. Some saints are able to do this one time in their life, some 9 times, some 99 times. Shaykh Sharafuddin (q) did it 19,999 times. But Shaykh AbdAllah (q) recited the King of Dhikrs twice on each breath. On every breath he breathed out he recited the entire Quran and all of its secrets. On every breath he breathed in, he recited the entire Quran and all of its secrets. He completed the Quran twice on each breath throughout his long life.

One day in 1973 CE he announced to his followers that the Prophet (sas) was calling him. He stopped eating and wrote his will. On Sunday, the 4th of Ramadan, 1393 AH, he left this world, much to the grief of his followers. He was buried beneath his small mosque on the mountain of Qasyun. He was placed lovingly in his grave by his dearest disciple, the one to whom he was leaving the light and secret of the Golden Chain, Shaykh Muhammad Nazim Adil al-Haqqani (q).

May Allah bless, an-Nabi (sas), Siddiq (ra), Salman (ra), Qasim (ra), Jafar (ra), Tayfur (q), Abul Hasan (q), Abu Ali (q), Yusuf (q), Abul Abbas al-Khidr (as), Abdul Khaliq (q), Arif (q), Mahmoud (q), Ali (q), Muhammad Baba as-Samasi (q), Sayyid Amir Kulal (q), Shah Bahauddin an-Naqshband (q), Alauddin (q), Ya'qub (q), UbaydAllah (q), Muhammad az-Zahid (q), Darwish Muhammad (q), Muhammad al-Amkanaki (q), Muhammad al-Baqi (q), Ahmad al-Faruqi (q), Muhammad Ma'sum (q), Sayfuddin (q), Nur Muhammad (q), Habib Allah (q), AbdAllah (q), Shaykh Khalid (q), Shaykh Ismail (q), Khas Muhammad (q), Shaykh Muhammad Effendi al-Yaraghi (q), Sayyid Jamaluddin al-Ghumuqi al-Husayni (q), Abu Ahmad as-Sughuri (q), Abu Muhammad al-Madani (q), Shaykh Sharafuddin ad-Daghestani (q), and Shaykh AbdAllah al-Faiz ad-Daghestani (q).

40
Shaykh Nazim Adil al-Haqqani (q)

Shaykh Nazim (q) is the keeper, in our time, of the light of the Prophet (sas) and the possessor of the cloak of mercy. He was decorated with the name al-Haqqani because he reached the station of the people of Truth. (Allahu Haqq: God is Truth.) He knows the purpose and value of each particle of God's creation. This enables him to accord to each its God-given right, not more and not less. He is the pole around which all living things turn, the master of the saints of the seven continents. Each of God's creatures, seen and unseen, known and unknown, is drawn to him, just as all rivers are drawn to the sea.

Shaykh Nazim (q) was born in the city of Larnaca on the island of Cyprus on the 26th of Shaban, 1340 AH, April 23, 1922 CE. A descendant of the Prophet (sas), he is also descended from the great saints, Jalaluddin Rumi (q) on his mother's side and AbdulQadir al-Jilani (q) on his father's side.

As a child his parents moved to the town of Nicosia where he grew up with his three older brothers and one sister. He had a childhood full of simple pleasures. He played and went to school with the other children. He delighted in the beauty of the natural world around him, the plants and flowers. He particulary enjoyed watching the ants and other small creatures.

But his dearest pleasure was to accompany his father to Larnaca to visit the mosque of Umm Hiram (rah), a companion of the Prophet (sas). Umm Hiram (rah) had been a beloved "Auntie" of the Prophet (sas). In her old age, for blessing, she had accompanied the Muslim army and died in Cyprus. A large slab of rock that she had admired before setting sail from Lebanon, flew across the ocean to hang, miraculously in mid-air, above her grave. Shaykh Nazim (q) developed a close spiritual relationship with her, like a grandson to his grandmother. He spent many childhood hours by her side.

Shaykh Nazim (q) attended school in Nicosia, speaking both Greek and Turkish, learning English as well. His fellow students recognized something special in their companion. Whenever they had a problem or difficult decision they asked him for his advice. They called him "the mufti," because of his serious, sincere and pious behaviour. He had a special talent for being able to explain the most complicated truths in simple, easy-to-understand ways.

His father sent him to the University in Turkey to study chemical engineering, but his heart was drawn to the Sufi masters he met in Istanbul. Every day he studied with excellence at the University. Every night he studied with devotion at the feet of the Shaykhs. Late at night, after the regular ferries had stopped, he would still find a small boat waiting just to take him across the Bosphorous to the company of his shaykhs.

Instead of continuing his engineering studies as his teachers wished, he devoted himself to religious studies and worship. His guides in Istanbul told him that they did not hold the key to his heart. He must go to Damascus to find his shaykh. It was in the middle of World War II and the Middle East was one of the battlegrounds. There was very little passenger traffic and crossing borders was difficult and dangerous. But nothing could keep Shaykh Nazim (q) from setting out for Damascus.

Everywhere he went he found people expecting him. The Prophet (sas) would appear in their dreams saying that his grandson was coming and that they must take good care of him. In Homs he spent one year in seclusion in the mosque where the great Companion of the Prophet (sas), Khalid ibn al-Walid (ra), is buried. He was unable, because of the war, to travel on. He used this time to improve his Arabic.

After a year and a half he finally arrived in Damascus. The city was under attack. The streets were empty and dark. He did not have an address but in a dream he had seen his

Shaykh for a moment, calling to him from a doorway. He vaguely remembered the look of the door and he searched for it up and down the deserted streets.

Finally he found it and knocked. Shaykh AbdAllah (q) opened the door immediately. He had been expecting him. He took him up to his prayer room. Outside Shaykh Nazim (q) could hear the sounds of airplanes, and bombs exploding. Inside he could see only light and peace. They prayed together and then Shaykh Nazim (q) saw the feet of a ladder descend onto his prayer carpet. The rungs of the ladder reached high into the heavens. Shaykh AbdAllah (q) took him step by step up this ladder, each rung of which represented a different spiritual station.

At last they reached the *Bayt al-Ma'mur*, the original, heavenly Ka'aba. Here they found the Prophet (sas) with all the Angels (ahums), Prophets (ahums) and Saints (qhum) about to make the morning prayer. There were two spaces on the right side of AbuBakr (ra) left open for them. The Prophet (sas) led the prayer. Shaykh Nazim (q) later said that the voice of the Prophet (sas), and his way of reciting the Quran, was the sweetest thing he had ever heard. After the prayer Shaykh Abdullah (q) introduced him to all the Prophets (ahums) and the Saints of the Golden Chain (qhum). All of them poured their secrets into his heart, accepting him into their exalted company.

After this they returned to Shaykh AbdAllah's (q) small room in the middle of Damascus, in the middle of the war. Shaykh AbdAllah (q) turned to face Shaykh Nazim (q) and his eyes began to change. First they glowed with a yellow light, then a red, then a white, then a green and then finally, a black light. With each color he gave Shaykh Nazim (q) the unique spiritual experiences that go with it.

Never had Shaykh Nazim (q) known anyone like Shaykh AbdAllah (q). He appeared to him to be more beautiful than words can describe. Light streamed from his face and forehead. The warmth of Divine Love poured from his heart. He knew that after years of searching he had finally found his master and never, ever wanted to leave him.

But having things the way you want them is not the way of the saints. Their way is the way Allah wants. Shaykh AbdAllah (q) turned to Shaykh Nazim (q) and ordered him to leave that very day. He must return to his homeland of Cyprus to guide his people. This was a most difficult test. It took Shaykh Nazim (q) more than a year and a half to even find his shaykh, and now, after only one night, he was being sent away. But spirituality is not just about prayer and dhikr. It is about putting the welfare of others above your own. It is about caring for and serving all of God's creatures.

However difficult it might have been, Shaykh Nazim (q) did not hesitate. He left immediately for Lebanon to try to find a boat sailing for Cyprus. Because of the war there was no fuel to power the motorboats. With great difficulty all he could find was a small sailboat. It took him seven days to reach Cyprus, a journey that normally took four hours. As soon as he set foot on shore, however, he felt his heart open. Shaykh AbdAllah (q) appeared before him and promised that as a consequence of his obedience they would never again be separated. Whenever Shaykh Nazim (q) turned his heart towards Shaykh AbdAllah (q), Shaykh AbdAllah (q) would be there.

Shaykh Nazim (q) was given the task of traveling and reminding. Some of the Muslim world was trying to throw away its heritage and its religion in order to follow the West and become "modern". In some countries, like Turkey and Cyprus, it became against the law even to practice Islam. Shaykh Nazim (q) traveled from town to town, his pointed green hat and wrapped turban a constant reminder of the ways of the Prophet (sas) that they were trying to discard. (The Prophet (sas) said that the turban is the crown of the Muslims, the more layers that are wrapped, the more blessings you receive.) He broke into every mosque the government had locked, climbed the minaret and called the people to prayer. He was arrested hundreds of times before the laws were finally changed.

Other countries in the Middle East had been torn apart by war and colonial occupation. Later Shaykh Nazim (q) was ordered to travel in Lebanon and Syria, stopping in every mosque to pray and to teach. He helped keep the tolerant and peaceful nature of true Islam alive when anger and politics were threatening to bury it forever.

Shaykh Sharafuddin (q) had predicted that one of his spiritual inheritors would travel to England and the West to introduce them also to the spiritual reality of Islam. Shaykh Abdullah (q) saw that Shaykh Nazim (q) was that one. Shaykh Nazim (q) began to travel to London every Ramadan. Here people from all over the globe, from Germany, Australia, Indonesia, America, Turkey, and Russia, all had the good fortune to meet him and kiss his hand. The Way he brought was so loving and so sane, so full of light and understanding that it brought healing and hope to people deadened by believing only in a material world.

He attracted Muslims who had forgotten their religion or had abandonned it for modern pleasures. He attracted Westerners who had found little guidance in the traditions of their birth. Shaykh Nazim (q) served for all of them as an example of sanity and beauty, truth and kindness. He welcomed them, fed them, listened to them, talked to them. He showed them a way out of their poverty of spirit, a way to approach God, a way to truly live life. He set an example of faith that knows no compromise and of love that accepts everyone.

Shaykh Nazim (q) is not just a guardian over people. The entire created world is under his care. Once he went to visit his daughter, Hajja Naziha, in Tripoli, Lebanon where she lived with her husband, Shaykh Hisham Kabbani. They kept a large birdcage on the balcony outside his room. Every morning after prayer Shaykh Nazim (q) would sit on the balcony watching the sunrise and listening to the hundreds of little paradise birds chirp and sing inside their cage.

After some time Shaykh Nazim (q) asked his daughter to open the door of the cage and let the birds go free. "Their freedom will bring them happiness and bring you blessing," he told her. All the little birds flew out, their wings making a sound like a breath long held and then suddenly released. They looked like the scattered bits of a rainbow sweeping the sky, singing in their joy.

There was a civil war going on in Lebanon at that time. Three weeks after this incident, a rocket hit the corner of the balcony just beside the empty birdcage. The rocket took a big bite out of the cement wall but the bomb inside it did not explode. If it had, the whole apartment building and all the people and animals in it, would have been destroyed. Instead, it fell harmlessly onto the pavement far below. One act of kindness and charity had saved the whole neighborhood and its inhabitants.

Some time later the brother of one of the Shaykh's students came to visit. He did not believe in God and certainly did not believe in the power of shaykhs. He listened to Shaykh Nazim (q) give a talk about the miraculous powers of the Prophet (sas) and how he could even bring the dead back to life. The man did not believe that such things were possible and he left the Shaykh's company stronger in doubt. He returned to his home. Outside his door he found the six or seven baby chicks that he had bought as pets for his children. They had all died and his wife had put them in a cardboard box and thrown them into the garbage. He was sad to see their soft, little bodies cold and limp. He said bitterly to himself, "Let the Shaykh bring these back to life." Then he entered his house and lay down to sleep.

Sometime in the middle of the night the man woke to the sound of chirping and scratching outside his window. He went to look and found all the fuzzy little chicks alive and hopping about in the box. His heart opened and he believed. First thing in the morning he went back to Shaykh Nazim (q) and took his hand. The Shaykh is the one who holds the key to your heart. Only he knows what will open its lock.

Now in his eighties, Shaykh Nazim (q) lives in an old-fashionned house in the small village of Lefke, Cyprus. He is no longer required to travel the world in order to bring people to the worship of their Creator. Instead the whole world now comes to him. At his table you will find men, women and children who have come to see him from areas bordering the North Sea, from Patagonia on the tip of South America, and from all places in between. Every single one of them is fed, housed, listened to and advised. They are all made to feel they are loved and cared for and above all, understood.

Before her death in 2005 his wife, Hajja Aminah (qha), or Hajja Anna as she was lovingly known, taught the women by her blessed example. She cooked for and served the shaykh and his guests with love and kindness. She inspired them with wonderful stories of the prophets and saints. She was a shining example of how to be a mother, a wife and a follower of the shaykh. She was a saint in her own right, and Shaykh Nazim's (q) dearest companion. Although all of the shaykhs in the Golden Chain are men they were supported and surrounded by strong, saintly women, as was the Prophet Muhammad (sas) himself.

The intimate details of the shaykh's household are a book open to visitors. They can see the principles by which he lives concretely demonstrated in all the small details of daily life. Vegetables are gathered from the market and farms. Those that were not sold, that vendors were going to throw away, are cooked first. Old bread that was not sold is brought to the Shaykh's door in trucks and creatively reinvented as appetizing delicacies. The Shaykh oversees all details of this process, ensuring that no bean is wasted, no leaf of *molokhia* forgotten on the stem. What is left goes to feed the farm animals or the dozens of small cats that patrol the house. He personally checks the garbage to make sure nothing usable is discarded. In a world where waste dominates, here there is no waste and no extravagance.

People speaking every language imaginable pack in together to pray and learn, their faces shining with happiness and their hands busy with useful work. They learn to be patient and polite with each other. They experience firsthand what it means to live in the manner of the Prophet (sas), where work and prayer combine to make a harmonious life. Most of them return to their faraway homes to tell others about what they experienced. The next year more people come to see for themselves.

Some people, however, stay and build lives around the Shaykh's house in Lefke. Each one does what he can to serve and support the work of the Shaykh. They are refugees from the world. Little by little Lefke is becoming like Rashadiya (see chapter 37) where every stone, every worm, and every heart is making dhikr, praising its Lord.

From this small village, Shaykh Nazim (q) watches over the whole world, with care and with mercy. When the big earthquake hit Istanbul in 1999 the television showed a woman being dug out of the rubble, miraculously unhurt, clutching a picture of the Shaykh to her heart. Many people have been cured of illness just by his prayer. Many childless couples have had babies after his blessing.

Although his ability to travel physically has been curtailed, he still travels spiritually. People have reported keeping company with him for many days while on Hajj. Others have heard him speak at important religious gatherings in European cities. All of these happened at the same time that his family and followers were sitting with him in his house in Cyprus.

He also has the ability to teach and to guide people through their dreams. What the Shaykh says to you in a dream is as true as what he says to you in person. One man, imprisoned in China for teaching the Quran, was guided in his escape to freedom by dreams of Shaykh Nazim (q). Only upon reaching safety in Turkey did he see a picture of the Shaykh in a newspaper article and find out who he was.

Shaykh Nazim's (q) days are spent caring for all his guests, seeing to their spiritual and physical needs. He talks to anyone who wants to talk to him and gives full attention to their concerns, no matter how trivial they seem. His nights are spent mostly in prayer and worship. He sleeps very little and only in short stretches of time. Although his meals are hearty, healthy, and abundant, he himself eats very little. Instead he spends the meal feeding and entertaining his guests. His prayerbeads never leave his hand as he continuously calls on his Lord and keeps count of his remembrance.

Shaykh Nazim (q) is the master of hearts. Streams of people from every corner of the earth flow, like many-colored rivers, to the ocean of love and truth which waits beyond his open door. We thank Allah for giving him to us as a light shining brightly in dark times. We pray that he stays with us for a very, very long time. And we trust that through our connection to him our hearts are connected to all the Shaykhs of the Golden Chain (qhums) and through them to our beloved Prophet (sas) and through him to the Divine Presence of Allah Almighty.

May Allah bless an-Nabi (sas), Siddiq (ra), Salman (ra), Qasim (ra), Jafar (ra), Tayfur (q), Abul Hasan (q), Abu Ali (q), Yusuf (q), Abul Abbas al-Khidr (as), Abdul Khaliq (q), Arif (q), Mahmoud (q), Ali (q), Muhammad Baba as-Samasi (q), Sayyid Amir Kulal (q), Shah Bahauddin an-Naqshband (q), Alauddin (q), Ya'qub (q), UbaydAllah (q), Muhammad az-Zahid (q), Darwish Muhammad (q), Muhammad al-Amkanaki (q), Muhammad al-Baqi (q), Ahmad al-Faruqi (q), Muhammad Ma'sum (q), Sayfuddin (q), Nur Muhammad (q), Habib Allah (q), AbdAllah (q), Shaykh Khalid (q), Shaykh Ismail (q), Khas Muhammad (q), Shaykh Muhammad Effendi al-Yaraghi (q), Sayyid Jamaluddin al-Ghumuqi al-Husayni (q), Abu Ahmad as-Sughuri (q), Abu Muhammad al-Madani (q), Shaykh Sharafuddin ad-Daghestani (q), Shaykh AbdAllah al-Faiz ad-Daghestani (q), and Shaykh Nazim al-Haqqani (q).

www.ingramcontent.com/pod-product-compliance
Lightning Source LLC
Chambersburg PA
CBHW051404070526
44584CB00023B/3280